HOPPING OVER THE RABBIT HOLE

HOPPING OVER THE RABBIT HOLE

HOW ENTREPRENEURS TURN FAILURE INTO SUCCESS

ANTHONY
SCARAMUCCI

WILEY

For Deidre,
AJ, Amelia,
Anthony, and Nicholas

Contents

Foreword

There was widespread panic in fall 2008 with the collapse of Lehman Brothers—the largest bankruptcy in history—but by late-winter/early-spring 2009, the bottom really fell out and there was widespread pessimism and gloom. By March 2009 the stock market was screeching to a 13-year bottom. The Federal Reserve was about to unleash record liquidity, but before that happened, many hedge funds went out of business and there was massive consolidation in the commercial and investment banking sectors. It felt like a precursor to the next great global recession.

There was a small firm named SkyBridge run by a guy that I had never met. His name was Anthony Scaramucci and from what I could tell, they had a small fund that was hobbled by the global financial crisis but they were trying to pretend that they were going to be okay. A partner there named Victor Oviedo reached out to me to see if I wanted to speak at their hedge fund conference, which they were calling the SALT (which stood for SkyBridge Alternatives) Conference. They wanted me on a panel to discuss the future.

"Why me?" I asked.

"Our industry is facing unprecedented turbulence and downturns, highlighted by dire forecasts and unnerving negativity. You, however, are an extreme optimist and we need a boost of positivity." Victor explained.

It would be another three years before I co-authored *Abundance: The Future is Better Than You Think*, but I was prepared to talk about a future where technological innovation would make it possible to provide health and wealth for everyone on the planet. With that premise in mind, I made the case about the abundant future to a dour group of delegates who were uncertain about the economy and its impact on their businesses. Yet, what none of us knew then was that we were at the beginning of an entrepreneurial adventure for SkyBridge and its founder Anthony Scaramucci.

I first met Anthony at that 2009 event and from the looks of him you wouldn't have known that he—and his business—were hurting. He had confidence and charisma, was a great public speaker, and the consummate salesman. But more importantly, he had a level of persistence and passion I rarely see.

What you will learn from *Hopping Over the Rabbit Hole* is that SkyBridge was teetering and was close to failing. Anthony kept a brave front and pushed on, and the insights he learned are told in the following pages in all their glory, in the most refreshingly honest and thoughtful fashion. I often fear reading autobiographical books about entrepreneurs since most sanitize the facts and forget their failures. Rich and successful people have a tendency to do that. The glory that they have found starts to distort their past in an effort to make their journey look effortless. You won't find any of that here. While the story hits rock bottom on a number of occasions, both the company and the culture never break, they bounce.

Anthony has written an honest appraisal of his firm and his own skills as an entrepreneur replete with personal anecdotes about human weakness and folly. He also loaded this book with advice. If you are starting a business and are buying this book as a roadmap or an inspirational tool, I would suggest that you read it with a highlighter except that you'd probably mark up every page. The material is that good—primarily because it is so honest and raw. You can feel the anxiety and fear of failure mixed in with the overconfidence and unbridled enthusiasm. Anthony grew up in a middle-class family, so while he had a decent upbringing and lifestyle, there was no safety net to fall onto if things went south. He tells his stories with a level of honesty and graciousness. You can feel his excitement but also his frailty and fear.

In September 2014, Anthony attended the Executive Program of Singularity University (SU), the Silicon Valley-based institution focused on exponential technologies that I co-founded with artificial intelligence legend (and Google's Chief Innovation Officer), Ray Kurzweil. His son AJ had previously attended SU's full 10-week Global Solutions Program (GSP) and he coaxed his dad to come out for the one-week intensive executive version. AJ would eventually go on to become a member of my Strike Force (an apprentice), but back then he was trying to open his father's eyes to the world of disruptive exponential technologies such as nanotechnology, virtual reality, and artificial intelligence. When I had the chance to connect with Anthony at SU and ask him the question I often chide New York financial types with, "Are you changing the world?" he responded quickly by saying, "No, not in the way you guys are." There was no false modesty in that statement, but he missed something big.

Truth be told, Anthony and SkyBridge were in fact transforming their industry. Hedge funds were primarily for the very wealthy or for the sophisticated institution. SkyBridge came along with a product that was able to bring the world of hedge fund investing to the mass affluent. Years ago, hedge fund managers were only taking large minimum investment checks. In some cases, the very best managers had a $10 or $15 million minimum investment. SkyBridge created a vehicle where investors only need to put up $25,000. This changed the landscape for the hedge fund community and he and his firm increased the number of people that could invest in these sorts of alternative investments. It also fits into the themes that I often write and speak about: the democratization of products and services that used to be reserved for the ultra-wealthy and are now being made available to the masses.

The life of the entrepreneur is typically only glamorous in hindsight. I often joke that many of my companies have been "overnight successes... after ten years of hard work." The daily grind has countless ups and downs, and far too many stressful decisions that hold the fate of a company and its employees in the balance. While we glorify the success stories in the media, rarely do we get a true glimpse of what is actually happening day to day. Anthony not only provides that here, but he is willing to share what he learned while eating humble pie and stumbling on the road to success.

That SALT conference that I attended in 2009—which was born from the failures of the 2008 global financial crisis—is now the leading event in the world of alternative investments. More than 2,200 people turn up at the Bellagio Hotel each May to immerse themselves in three and a half days of learning, networking, and entertainment. SkyBridge had created a community that connects Hollywood, Wall Street, Washington DC, technology, and biotechnology in a way that leaves people mesmerized.

While I don't wish setbacks on any of my friends, what I am confident of is if SkyBridge or Anthony ever get into a rut again, something very positive will come out of it. By reading this book you will learn the intimate details and lessons of how Anthony and his colleagues snatched victory from what looked like an imminent defeat. Being an entrepreneur is not easy, and being an entrepreneur with bold dreams takes guts.

I encourage you to turn these pages and find out what drives people to dream big. What mindset enables someone to start with nothing and shoot for the stars, all the while refusing to give up where other mere mortals accept defeat. My guess is you will find yourself somewhere here in this story and by doing so it will radically transform your self and your business.

PETER H. DIAMANDIS, MD
Founder and Executive Chairman, XPRIZE Foundation
Founder and Executive Chairman, Singularity University
Author of *New York Times* bestsellers *Abundance* and *BOLD*

Introduction

T here is no way around it. Business can be brutal. Consider this: Half of all businesses will vanish in only their first year of operation. Eighty percent of new businesses will have failed by their fifth anniversary. At the 10-year mark, 96% will have failed. Only 4% survive a decade! And that doesn't mean you are out of the weeds. Heck, even businesses that have been around 100 years have collapsed (Remember Lehman Brothers?). And yet, for those that find a way to break through the limitations, there are not only economic rewards but deep emotional and spiritual ones as well.

Business owners are Gladiators because the longer they play the game, the greater statistical chance their business will die. It takes a unique psychology to step into the arena knowing the odds. Some might say you need to be a little crazy. But Gladiators don't subscribe to statistics. They simply step up to the challenge and embrace the level of commitment and sacrifice required—day in, day out, rain or shine. There is a kinship that all entrepreneurs share because we know what it takes—Anthony knows what it takes.

This book captures the essence of the Gladiator spirit with Anthony's own inspiring and profound story of reinventing his business after the financial crises to become Ernst and Young's 2011 *Entrepreneur of the Year.* I know you'll appreciate his candid approach to discussing his own dark days. And yet, he didn't let the dark days define him. He used those challenges as fuel to find a way. Fuel to grow. Fuel to learn. Fuel to think outside the box. Anthony is an extraordinary example of what's possible when you won't tolerate failure or excuses within yourself or others involved in your mission.

So what does it take to become truly successful in business, to grow your company and build true wealth for yourself, your shareholders, and your employees? The answer to this question is simple yet profound. You must become obsessed with one thing: figuring out how you can do more for others than anyone else could possibly imagine! Finding a way to continually add more value. That is precisely why Anthony's SALT conference is off the charts each and every year.

Motive does matter, and if you can remember to fall in love with your client, not your product or service, you are going to win in the long run. Products and services will be disrupted and replaced, but if you always strive to find unique and innovative ways to meet your customers' needs, you will create raving fans, not just satisfied clients. Satisfied clients will jump ship while raving clients will be with you until the end.

Over the past 39 years, I have had the privilege of working with hundreds of thousands of business owners, from time tested billionaires to those just beginning the journey. One thing I know for sure: 80 percent of success is psychology and 20 percent is mechanics. You can teach someone every strategy, but if their mind is dominated by fear, overwhelming anxiety and anger, they will self-destruct or leave a wake of destruction behind them. In the pages ahead, Anthony outlines some killer strategies but more importantly, he reveals the winning psychology.

You have the opportunity to extract as much wisdom from these pages as you possibly can because you're about to learn from a man who walks his talk. I wish for you challenges, enormous growth, and great success.

With Deep Respect,
TONY ROBBINS

Chapter 1

The Shape of Things to Come
Seeing Around Corners

"You may not realize it when it happens, but a kick in the teeth may be the best thing in the world for you."

—*Walt Disney*

"I want to thank my good friend Andy for putting this conference together," Steve Wynn told the packed ballroom at the Encore Hotel. "These are very tough times. And it takes a lot of courage for him and his team to be out here—in Las Vegas—putting on this magnificent event."

The crowd erupted in applause. But I was distracted. My body tensed up as I looked over at my business partner.

"Did Steve Wynn just call me Andy?" I asked with a plastered smile on my face.

"Andrew," he paused pensively. "Andrew, on behalf of Las Vegas, I want to thank you."

More applause.

Yup, he definitely got my name wrong. In front of 500 people. A group that included industry thought leaders, hedge fund billionaires, prominent investors, and friends. People who—until that moment—knew me as Anthony Scaramucci. Maybe the Mooch. Certainly not Andy; and, never as Andrew.

But, it didn't matter. After all, at that very moment I was witnessing what could only be considered a minor miracle.

■ ■ ■

It was May 2009. Steve Wynn had just made the opening remarks at the inaugural SkyBridge Alternatives (SALT) Conference. His newly opened Encore hotel was opulent, filled with celebrity restaurants, gorgeous bars, and an abundance of fiery-red gaming tables, all of which stood empty as the Great Recession wreaked havoc on America's adult playground.

If you told me that just two months earlier I would be standing in Las Vegas, listening to Steve Wynn speak to 500 members of the alternative investment industry about my firm's courageous audacity to host an event during an economic crisis, I would have said you were nuts.

Flashback to March 2009. The Standard & Poor's (S&P) 500 had hit rock bottom. The world, it seemed, was on the verge of collapse. And, I feared that my investment firm—SkyBridge Capital—would soon be among the casualties. I founded SkyBridge—an alternative investment management company, focused on seeding and partnering with emerging managers and mentoring Wall Street's next generation of Wall Street's entrepreneurs—in 2005. And now, just four years later, I feared it I was going to lose my business—and worse, my clients' money. As redemptions starting flooding in, I knew that if we didn't do something proactive, something aggressive, something strategic, we weren't going to be SkyBridge—we were going to be "NoBridge." I was beginning to feel hopeless as my partners and I faced an all-but-certain death. I wasn't sure if SkyBridge was going to survive.

I was scared. Actually, I was terrified. But I was *not* panicked. Panic is a different emotion. Panic implies that there is no rational thought taking place. That we are frozen and incapable of adjusting. Powerless to logic, and subject to seemingly unthinkable behavior.

Amid the chaos, my business partner Victor Oviedo came to me with an idea. He explained that a business acquaintance was running an alternative investing summit in Las Vegas and was struggling to fill seats. In addition, he continued, many major financial institutions were scrambling to cancel their upcoming conferences and Vegas-related business travel after President Obama sounded the warning bells on Wall Street and corporate America, saying, "You can't take a trip to Las Vegas or go down to the Super Bowl on the taxpayer's dime." Against this seemingly dire backdrop, Victor had a plan.

"What if SkyBridge threw a hedge fund conference in Vegas?" he suggested.

I smirked . . . thinking he was joking. But, by the look on his face, I could tell he was serious.

He excitedly continued, "We'll call it the SkyBridge Alternatives Conference, or 'SALT.'"

Victor is an extremely creative and strategic person. He sees around corners and anticipates trends before other people do. He's also one of the most deliberate people I know . . . and I mean that in a good way. He doesn't open his mouth unless he has something important to say. He doesn't throw things to the wall to see what sticks; rather, he is thoughtful and measured in his approach to business. With that in mind, I thought it was rather strange that—as our business was failing—he would come to me pitching the idea of a glorified party in Sin City.

I continued to look at him in utter disbelief. A conference? In Vegas? During an economic crisis? What would our clients say? After all, we were in the seeding business; not the conference business. Besides, we could barely make payroll and were maybe two phone calls away from closing up shop—how were we going to finance a conference? The idea—even to me—was outlandish . . . bizarre . . . crazy! Or was it?

"Come on, Vic," I said. But as the words fell out of my mouth, I knew we were on to something. This was the time to take a calculated risk. This was the time to ignore political rhetoric and bring together members of the financial community to identify solutions that would allow us all to capitalize on tomorrow's opportunities. This was the time to dive in with both feet and hop—actually, leap—over the rabbit hole. Suddenly, Victor's idea was beginning to make sense. If fact, the contrarian in me suddenly found it brilliant!

If we didn't change the way we were doing business, we wouldn't even have a business. We needed to think outside the box. We needed to be creative; adaptable; entrepreneurial. Reinvent ourselves. We needed to play offense, while the rest of the industry was playing defense. And while there was no tangible relationship between the conference business and the hedge fund business, I did, however, recognize the void in the marketplace as well as SkyBridge's need to move in another direction.

It was becoming more and more clear to me—this conference would give SkyBridge the opportunity to send a message to our clients, our competitors, and the industry that we were hopeful about SkyBridge's future . . . that we were hopeful about Wall Street's—and America's—future. We'd be instilling confidence, optimism, and perseverance—something no government official, policymaker, or central bank was willing to do in 2009. We would be sending a message that we may have encountered a roadblock, but we were going to come together to overcome it. And as a firm, SkyBridge would be leading this charge.

As the founder of SkyBridge, I also saw SALT as a huge asset to help us grow—actually, save—our business. If we were going to survive the Great Recession, the only way to get the message out was to operate on the balls of our feet, not our heels. Call it "fake it 'til you make it." Call it "smoke and mirrors." Call it whatever you want. The message was clear—we were not going down without a fight.

Having worked in the industry for 20+ years, I also knew that Wall Street was all about building trust, goodwill, and relationships. And I knew that there was no better way to develop meaningful relationships than by taking the time to meet prospective and existing clients face-to-face. As such, I firmly believed that SALT would introduce SkyBridge to a critical mass of potential investors and peer managers. Furthermore, it would be an opportunity to raise our profile and separate us from our peers. In my mind, SALT had morphed from a nonsensical idea to a no-brainer. A strategy to save our business. But, now I had to convince my partners.

■ ■ ■

Two months before the proposed first annual SALT Conference, I gathered my partners together in our oversized conference room so I could present the idea.

"Gentlemen," I said as we began the partner's meeting. "We have an opportunity in front of us. An opportunity to start a conference. The SkyBridge Alternatives Conference. SALT. It will serve as an industry platform. One that will introduce us to a ton of potential investors, while raising the profile of SkyBridge Capital."

Silence.

Absolute silence.

"Besides, what is the worst that can happen?" I continued, hoping to inject some levity in the room, "At least we will have a going-out-of-business party."

As expected, my other partners did not exactly share my enthusiasm. In fact, they thought Victor and I were completely crazy. Our business was on life support. And this event would cost money that we didn't need to spend. They pleaded: "How is this glorified going-away party going to contribute to our bottom-line?" "What would investors say?" "Besides, do we even know how to put together a conference . . . and in less than two months?" But the more my team kept telling me it was too risky, the more the contrarian in me believed in its promise.

Well, as you can imagine, the vote was five against two—and I bet you can guess the culprits of those two lone votes. There we had it. No conference. No Las Vegas. And, perhaps, no SkyBridge.

I am a team player. I believe in consensus. I believe in a democratic corporate practice, where checks and balances are in place in order to ensure that my partners and I are collectively reaching our business objectives and responsibly propelling the organization while serving the needs of our clients. But, at that moment in time, the stakes were just too high. Our business—and, some would argue, the industry— was on the brink of failure. Besides, I truly believed that the conference was the key to reinvigorating our business—that, and I maintained control through our corporate governance agreement.

"Gentlemen, I hear your concerns." I paused. "Thank you for your vote. We're doing it anyway."

(There was a famous cabinet vote during the Civil War where Lincoln called for the vote: "9 nays, 1 aye, the ayes have it." Well, it sort of went like that. In times of distress, real leadership means making bold—sometimes unilateral—decisions.)

And with that we started planning.

■ ■ ■

Truth be told, we had less than two months to gather the relevant industry players, plan a comprehensive agenda, create a web site, and produce a unique event . . . something that would grab the market's attention. Perhaps more overwhelming was the fact that my lean team had never planned a conference—let alone an event—in their entire lives . . . and we still had our day jobs.

Remember, we were all in the financial services business; not the event-planning industry. What the hell did we know about throwing an event . . . let alone an entire conference! But one thing we all had in common was that we had all been to tons of conferences throughout our careers and understood the needs of the audience as we—ourselves—were often in their seats. And so it hit us—we knew that SALT needed to be a conference *we* would all want to attend. It couldn't be some run-of-the-mill event nor a vendor expo where there was an overabundance of service suppliers hounding asset managers and investors on their way to the bathroom. It needed to be a forum where professionals were exposed to relevant and insightful editorial content, while providing them with opportunities to build meaningful relationships that would help their businesses grow. We wanted the audience to be properly composed of check writers and asset managers, with the best and brightest from Wall Street, Washington, and beyond. In order to reach these objectives, we knew that we needed head-turning names at the top of the speaker docket.

My first call was to Bob Miller, the former governor of Nevada. Having known his son, Ross—who was Nevada's secretary of state as well as a friend of the firm—I was put in touch with Governor Miller. It was a strategic first move, as I knew his support was integral in pulling off an event in the economically devastated state of Nevada. Furthermore, he was also on the board of Wynn Resorts, and—perhaps most importantly—he was closely acquainted with the man we hoped would be our keynote speaker at the first SALT Conference: Michael Milken.

I'll admit it. I have a man crush on Michael Milken. The guy was—and still is—a hero of mine. Often said to have "revolutionized modern capital markets," he is an entrepreneurial genius whose brilliance gave birth to the modern age of finance. Perhaps more importantly, he has also changed the face of medicine and is saving lives through his tireless efforts and formation of his Prostate Cancer Foundation and Faster Cures. Milken's approach to life and business represented the type of out-of-the-box mentality I was trying to instill at SkyBridge and impart at SALT.

With the help of Governor Miller, I was able to get Milken on the phone. And then something strange happened to me. I suddenly grew unbelievably nervous . . . intimidated even.

"Mr. Milken," I said. "Let me say that it is an honor to speak with you." I rarely get flustered, but I was definitely nervous.

"Call me Mike," he replied, immediately putting me at ease.

I explained the goals of SALT and its objectives and why we chose to hold it in Vegas. He interjected intermittently, with insightful questions and clarifying statements.

And, suddenly, I found myself not asking—but declaratively stating to my idol—that I'd like him to be SALT's inaugural keynote speaker.

Dead air.

A pregnant pause that felt like an hour, but probably was less than two seconds.

"Sure. I'd love to," Mike said. "And I'd like to invite you to attend my Global Conference, too. And, of course, make a donation to my foundation as a gesture of goodwill."

Little did I know this phone call would spark the beginning of a terrific relationship. To this day, Mike remains one of my most trusted advisers and mentors. He is my first phone call if a family member has a serious health issue and a true confidant. And, in retrospect, this episode is also an important reminder that we need to put our egos on the floor, get outside of our comfort zones, and push ourselves, while maintaining some level of gracious audacity.

With Mike Milken keynoting the event, he humbly suggested that Steve Wynn—the godfather of the American luxury hotel and casino industry—provide the introduction to his keynote remarks. At that time, he had just opened the Encore Las Vegas, which was the venue for the conference.

With Milken and Wynn on board, suddenly the task of completing a two-and-a-half-day agenda—and populating it with relevant headliners—came together nicely.

We secured Governor Oscar B. Goodman, Mayor of the city of Las Vegas; Dick Gephardt, former Democratic House majority leader and member of the U.S. House of Representatives representing Missouri; General Wesley Clark, former NATO supreme allied commander; and

Harvey Pitt, former chairman of the U.S. Securities and Exchange Commission. From there, we rounded out the agenda with members of the alternative asset industry who participated on panels that discussed the state and future of the economy and hedge funds.

In the meantime, Victor, Jason Wright—a senior partner and head of marketing at SkyBridge—and I focused our efforts on filling those empty seats and financing the event. We hit the phones . . . aggressively. We called every relevant player in the industry in order to gather a critical mass of prominent investors and asset managers. Having attended numerous conferences ourselves, we took a portfolio manager's asset allocation approach to composing the SALT delegation and strove for a 2:1 investor-to-manager ratio with a low number of service providers. We also approached each of the major banks' prime brokerage and cap intro teams, encouraging them to selectively invite their hedge fund clients to attend. In exchange, we offered each bank a bespoke sponsorship package, which enabled them to provide their clients with exclusive access to prominent speakers and networking events throughout the entire conference. Lastly, we invited a select number of academics, nonprofit leaders, and media personalities.

With only days to go before SALT, we had somehow managed to register approximately 500 people. To this day, I am not sure how it happened . . . and, I would be lying if I told you we envisioned the positive impact SALT would have on SkyBridge. But with that, we packed up and headed to Las Vegas. It was show time.

■■■

The big day arrived on May 9, 2009. The ballroom was packed. Wynn took the stage to thunderous applause. His pearly whites seemed to shine even brighter on stage, his deep voice resonating thanks to flawless acoustics in his brand new venue. Talk about fearless. If there was a financial crisis going on, you couldn't tell from Wynn's body language. Cool and collected, he strutted out and winked at the crowd. Here was a guy who had just opened up a billion-dollar resort smack dab in the middle of the worst financial crisis in 70 years, and he couldn't have looked more relaxed.

He stood in front of the SkyBridge Capital branded podium and—after thanking Andrew . . . I mean, me—proceeded to tell the story of the first time he met Milken.

It was 1978. A 36-year-old Steve Wynn wanted to build a grand hotel in Atlantic City, which—at the time—seemed destined to rival Vegas as America's favorite gambling destination. But, Wynn had no money. No investors. His friend, Stan Zax, suggested he meet with his cousin, Mike Milken, in Los Angeles to discuss the project.

Upon arriving at Milken's LA offices with Zax, Wynn cumber-somely hobbled around the lobby, as he had just broken his foot four days prior and was on crutches. Sensing his uncomfortableness, a young man in a golf polo and casual jeans approached him and Zax and sug-gested that they go into a conference room.

Wynn obliged and immediately rested his feet on the large table. The young man kindly offered Wynn a drink.

"Diet Cola would be great," Wynn promptly replied.

As the man left the room, Wynn turned to Zax and said, "I can't wait to meet this genius cousin of yours."

Without missing a beat, Zax responded, "You just did."

Amid a roar of laughter, Wynn proceeded to tell the audience how Milken changed his life. How Milken gave him the confidence to transform from a young, green, and inexperienced professional, who had a narrow strip of knowledge about a certain thing—in his case, a gambling hall called the Golden Nugget—into one of the biggest names in the gaming industry.

"'One day,'" Wynn recalled Milken telling him "'One day, you will be able to pick up the phone and borrow a billion dollars from people who trust you.' It was truly an education."

Milken would go on to finance some of Wynn's most iconic hotels. Together, the two changed the face of the luxury casino and gaming industry. In the process, they also transformed the Las Vegas strip into a high-end destination and family resort, consequently creating a metropolis burgeoning with middle-class jobs, great schools, and top-notch hospitals.

The speech struck a chord with me as I stood off stage. It made me think about where I was in my business. I, too, was at a crossroads. I wanted to grow SkyBridge beyond its narrow parameters. I wanted to change the face of the industry. I wanted to try something big, bold, and different I just wasn't sure how.

"Ladies and gentlemen," he concluded, "my teacher, my friend, and the most brilliant guy I've ever known, Michael Milken."

If Wynn's speech was inspiring, Milken's was downright mesmer- izing. He provided insightful, thought-provoking, and encouraging commentary on the state of the economy, showcasing his trademark contrarian way of thinking. He noted how the brightest investment opportunities often emerge when things seem darkest. To illustrate this point, he flashed the audience back to the late 1980s and talked about the collapse of the junk bond market and how investors with the presence of mind not to panic ultimately realized the opportunity of a lifetime. He then drew a correlation to the current market conditions and—against conventional wisdom and political rhetoric—encouraged investors to be uber-bullish. I could see heads in the crowd nodding as he spoke. They could not have been more engaged.

(By the way, Milken was right . . . again. At the time, little did we know that we were about to embark on one of the greatest bull market runs of all time.)

After Milken's speech, Wynn pulled me aside, this time getting my name right. As he patted my shoulder, he congratulated me for ignor- ing the naysayers and putting together a stellar, educational conference during an economic recession. He continued, "And, I thank you for helping Vegas, too. After the president slammed us, we have gotten a bad rap. But, what he doesn't get is just how many middle-class peo- ple depend on events like this. We have maids and bellhops who need these conferences, and it speaks to what you guys are about over there."

He could not have been more right.

The night after the conference ended, I headed over to the SW Steakhouse for a celebratory dinner with Victor and the SkyBridge team. Despite being a couple hundred thousand in the red, we felt pretty good about what we had just pulled off.

"This was a success," I told the team, hoisting a glass of red wine to toast. "Now how do we build on this for next year?"

It seemed like an obvious—yet, an audacious—question because we didn't know if there would even be a next year at SkyBridge . . . let alone another SALT Conference. And while we were encouraged by the success of SALT, we didn't fully grasp what we had created in just two months.

I felt an inevitable sense of dread the moment I boarded the plane back to New York. Remember, it was May 2009. The fact that we threw a killer conference and congregated some of the brightest minds in finance to identify solutions for economic recovery didn't negate the fact that the immediate global financial outlook seemed dire and SkyBridge's future remained uncertain. We didn't know what the next day would bring.

Entranced by Milken's words, I knew now more than ever that it was time to pivot and redefine ourselves. But, as what? Third-party marketers? Advisers? Conference organizers?

■ ■ ■

2010 proved to be a big year for us. A year that answered that question in ways I wouldn't have imagined at the time.

Through a series of bold and strategic strokes, our small firm acquired Citigroup's Alternative Investments Hedge Funds Management Group. No longer a pure seeding firm, we were now heading into the fund of hedge funds industry, and were about to quadruple in size . . . and staff.

As a result, the SALT Conference was about to take on an even greater meaning for us. In 2009, we just wanted people to know we weren't going out of business. Now, in 2010, we wanted people to recognize our brand as a household name. It was our coming-out party.

■ ■ ■

The stakes were high. Amid these negotiations, the SkyBridge team went into "SALT mode." Remember, we were investment and marketing professionals who still had our day jobs. And, as you know, the financial services industry is notoriously competitive, brutal, and unforgiving. SkyBridge was no different. Ten to twelve hour days were the norm. Planning SALT took it to another level. It was a seven-day-a-week, 24-hour-a-day meat grinder.

As part of the planning process, Victor and I established a creative content team. The goal was to identify relevant speakers in the industry and then organize them into themed panels. In a lot of ways, we functioned as television producers, figuring out the optimal rhythm and flow of the conference.

During this creative process, I began to see SALT a little bit differently and suddenly went into overdrive brainstorming ways in which we could elevate the editorial content of the conference's program. We needed to make the event about more than just alternative investing. We needed to expose our audience to lively discussions and debates on the world's most pressing issues. We needed to push the envelope, be provocative, be aspirational, be forward-thinking. Most of all, we needed bigger speakers . . . icons and influencers like Michael Milken.

"We need more than just money managers and financial advisors," I said to my team. "We need to think out-of-the-box and identify relevant speakers who are industry decision makers, who represent solutions, who are forward thinking. SALT can't just be about making money. It needs to be about leadership. It needs to be about," I paused for a second, searching for the right word: "*excellence.*"

And, I knew exactly who to get.

"I want one of the best public speakers in the world," I told my team in one of our planning meetings. "I want Bill Clinton."

President Clinton is another one of my personal heroes. Yes, I am a Republican, but I admire him and all great leaders regardless of party lines. His story—raised by his mom and an alcoholic stepfather in a poor, rural Arkansas town only to reach the highest office in the land—was an inspirational testament to the can-do spirit of the American people. Democrats revere him. Republicans respect him. And, despite how one may feel about some of his policies—it's impossible to deny his undeniable intelligence, ability to connect with people, and soulful charisma.

"How are we going to get him?" Victor asked, quizzically. "Do you really think a former president of United States is going to travel to Las Vegas and participate in a hedge fund conference?"

Probably not, but I had a secret weapon: Rick Lerner. Perhaps one of my closest friends, Rick was my college roommate at Tufts University. Upon graduation, he went to work at the White House during the Clinton administration and is now a successful private banker at Goldman Sachs.

"Hey, Rick," I exclaimed into my Blackberry, "I need a favor. I need to figure out a way to get to Bill Clinton to speak at SALT. Do you still have any contacts from your White House days that could help?"

I could hear him chuckling on the other end of the phone.

"Come on, Rick." I continued. "It would be huge. A game changer."

"If you want to get to Bill, you have talk to Doug," Rick told me.

Rick immediately put me in touch with Douglas J. Brand— President Clinton's former chief adviser and special assistant, who later went on to shape Clinton's post-presidency legacy and build the Clinton Global Initiative. Considered by many as Clinton's gatekeeper, he forged an unusually tight bond with the former president. Those who have seen the relationship up-close describe it more as more father-son than president-aide.

In any case, after a few e-mail exchanges back and forth, Doug and I arranged to speak by phone. As I had done just a year prior with

Milken, I told him about SALT and how we'd be honored to have former president Clinton provide the keynote address. Doug immediately gave me his blessing and put me in direct touch with the former president's speaking agency.

One discussion later and we got the former president of the United States to speak at SALT!

"We got Clinton," I said to Victor. "It's on."

Clinton's participation acted as a tractor beam for other high-profile guests. Knowing that my friend—Marc Lasry, legendary hedge fund manager and founder of Avenue Capital—was a Clinton advocate and acquaintance, I quickly gave him a call. Not only did he agree to speak on a SALT panel, but he even flew out and dined with Clinton while at the conference.

From there, we secured additional hedge fund titans, including Citadel's Ken Griffin, York Capital's Jamie Dinan, and Highbridge Capital's Glenn Dubin. We booked economic legends such as Austan Goolsbee, Nouriel Roubini, and Jeremy Siegel. And political leaders, such as Governor Mitt Romney and—of course—President Clinton. Michael Milken also agreed to come back and provide a keynote on "Unprecedented Times, Unprecedented Opportunities."

To fulfill my out-of-the-box mandate, we also secured Frank Abagnale—the subject of Steven Spielberg's 2002 movie *Catch Me if You Can*. Having seen him speak at an event a few months earlier, we immediately knew his story would make a great addition to the SALT lineup as his honestly and bluntness about his own personal shortcomings were so compelling. (As a side note, many attendees—to this day—single out Abagnale's lunch presentation as their favorite SALT highlight.)

All told, we assembled over 100 speakers—the GDP of a several small nations. An eclectic mix of world leaders, renowned investors, and leading economists.

■ ■ ■

The 2010 SALT Conference was shaping up as a crucial event for us, and not just because of the Citigroup deal or resurgent stock market. CNBC was considering covering it.

Through my good friend, Gary Kaminsky, I met CNBC fireball producer Susan Krakower, who told me the network would cover the conference on two conditions: I agreed to sign on as an exclusive network contributor and I lined up big guests for CNBC's exclusive coverage while her team was on the ground to cover the event.

"And not just the same people I see on CNBC day-in-day-out, Anthony!" Krakower screamed at me over dinner at the Core Club; for some reason, she always emphasized my name at the end. Susan and I clicked instantly. Now working at SkyBridge, she remains one of the most creative and brutally honest people I've ever met. She's also one of the loudest. "And you better up your game on TV. You're too soft. Kick it up. And get me big guests," she exclaimed. "I want to make this big."

CNBC's coverage of the conference helped to take SALT to another level. And, the network wasn't just going to cover it. They were sending David Faber and Maria Bartiromo—two of the network's biggest names—to broadcast live from the event. If anyone doubted we were for real, CNBC's presence put that notion to bed. SALT would become the news, and people—no matter who you are—love to be close to where news is happening. It was the type of advertising money couldn't buy as the discussions at SALT would be unfolding on one of the biggest financial news channels for the entire world to see.

■ ■ ■

It's hard to identify, in real time, the line between faking it and making it. But during the planning of the 2010 SALT Conference, I felt like we had surely crossed it. The success was starting to feel real, and it was unfolding on television for the entire world to see.

It was time to deliver. CNBC would be broadcasting, Wall Street would be watching, and the market would be talking. We couldn't mess up this opportunity.

■ ■ ■

I called Victor. I wanted SALT to have the look and feel of a heavy-weight boxing match. Reading about it in the *Wall Street Journal* wasn't enough. You *needed* to be there. And if you were at home watching it on CNBC, you needed to see it all.

"No more tiny plasma screens . . . we need to think big," we told our production team.

You see, we simply didn't have the funds to spend on AV elements at the first SALT Conference One year later, I knew we needed something bigger to showcase our brand for the entire world to see.

"A wall of video screens," I said, "screens like they have at sporting events in major stadiums. Screens that boldly state 'SkyBridge' and showcase our brand."

■ ■ ■

When we sent over the final SALT 2010 agenda, the CNBC producers were thrilled. Not only did the speakers generate headlines by the hour, but we were making finance seem accessible, transparent, and—perhaps, even—sexy. SALT was the place to see and be seen. Yes, it had a festive atmosphere, but there was real learning taking place. You also never knew who you would run into.

And that was the point. SALT trafficked in excellence, but what the conference was really about was access. Information is everywhere. And in the era of smartphones, it's become even more of a commodity. What people really want is context for all this information. They want insight delivered in a fun and digestible format. SALT provided that experience.

At the conclusion of the second annual SALT Conference, my team and I gathered for a celebratory dinner at Rao's. While the mood after the previous year's conference was cautious optimism, this time is was unbridled euphoria. As we dined on meatballs—which almost tasted as delicious as my Nana's—we knew we had created something very special. Not only had we helped transform the narrative about the financial industry and American economy, we helped its members establish new business relationships while engaging in cutting-edge discussions about the future of our industry, the global economy, and societal issues. In addition, SALT—or, more specifically, the ideals underlying it—would springboard our business into the future. Now we had a platform to promote our brand, demonstrate our expertise within the industry, and build relationships with both existing and potential clients.

■ ■ ■

I'm a firm believer in the idea that you're either moving forward or backward. You're either growing in confidence or swelling with hubris. The moment you become complacent is the moment you lose your edge. There is always somebody working harder than you, and there are always copycats ready to take the model you've built and make it better.

After our success in 2010, I told my team that we couldn't rest on our laurels. We needed to grow, scale, and evolve. And while we always aimed to break even on the event—and almost never do—we needed to create a business model that enabled us to secure more prominent and diverse speakers. Public figures and thought leaders who were leaders in their field and changing the way business was done. And, while the core agenda would stay true to the tenets of macroeconomic issues, geopolitical debates, and investment themes for the year ahead, we needed to strategically weave insights from prominent actors, athletes, and technology leaders into the event's tapestry. We wanted to associate the SkyBridge and SALT brands with excellence, with success, with relevancy. And we wanted to have fun while we were doing it. Where one minute you could hear David Tepper's market-moving view on the stock market and the next you could hear Magic Johnson discuss the similarities between sports and entrepreneurship.

Over the next five years, SALT would evolve from an alternative investments conference to a forum for alternative thinking. An international experience that attracts an eclectic array of prominent thought leaders from the interesting worlds of finance, politics, public policy, science, entertainment, and philanthropy. An experience designed to motivate and inspire, to educate and entertain, to move markets, and to grow business . . . and, a place—of course—to have fun.

Little did I know just how big things were about to get.

■ ■ ■

CNBC's wall-to-wall media coverage was doing more than just getting the word out on SALT. It was making me a bit of a TV star as well. It's funny, when I was at Goldman, I used to make fun of people who were on television all the time. "That dude's a clown," I'd often mumble at the screen. There was probably some jealousy in that statement, although I didn't fully realize it at the time. I was never a TV person. For the first 20+ years of my career, I anxiously avoided the bright lights. I only started to dabble in television because I thought some media exposure could help SkyBridge by instilling confidence in our clients, who would watch me on a financial television show and perceive me as an industry expert. And, it worked . . . People were starting to learn about our firm. Our name was getting out there. SkyBridge appeared to be a bigger deal than we really were. And, over time, the illusion became the reality, and suddenly, before I knew it, we had become leading players in the alternative investments space.

■ ■ ■

The success of SALT—in conjunction with my appearances on CNBC—helped raise SkyBridge's profile, but what happened next was something I never could have imagined. While I knew the conference had become a massive networking event for the hedge fund industry, I didn't fully realize how much the mainstream public was paying attention.

Oliver Stone called. He wanted to put me in his next movie, the long-awaited sequel to *Wall Street*. Through a mutual acquaintance, he asked if we could meet to talk about his next project. A week later, I was sitting in Stone's New York office reviewing parts of the script with Josh Brolin and Shia LaBeouf. In return, I asked Stone if he would take a look at a book I was currently writing that combined the themes of maintaining your moral compass with achieving financial security and professional success.

Not only did he read the manuscript, but he endorsed it and wrote the foreword. Kelly O'Connor—my brilliant editor, who now works at SkyBridge—suggested we integrate the Gordon Gekko name into the title. At first, I was hesitant. The name Gordon Gekko is synonymous with Wall Street douchebags, and the book was actually about the importance of rejecting materialistic values. But, Kelly won out with clever wordplay.

"We'll call it *Goodbye Gordon Gekko: How to Find Your Fortune without Losing Your Soul*," she suggested. "Remember, the book is about moving past that era. It's the perfect title."

Stone agreed, and soon after offered me a small cameo in *Wall Street 2: Money Never Sleeps* where I played myself at a fundraising event. Perhaps more importantly, he featured the SkyBridge logo prominently in the scene, further raising the awareness of our brand throughout the world.

Despite the good-natured ribbing from a few of my Wall Street buddies, I knew this out-of-the-box thinking was the exact type of thing I needed to do in order to differentiate the SkyBridge brand and make it a household name. And besides, the whole experience could not have been more enjoyable . . . and left me with some great stories to tell.

Before I knew it, I found myself on a flight to Cannes for the movie's premiere. I was seated five rows behind Michael Douglas. I was more excited than a five-year-old at Disney World. I brought along a copy of my brand new book, which I coyly handed to its factious namesake.

"Anthony! This is so great. Thank you," Douglas said, in his most convincing acting job to date.

He sat down and opened the book. As the plane took off, I was dying to know what he thought of it. After we reached a cruising altitude, I walked over to his seat. He was in a Stage 9 deep REM sleep, his mouth agape and the copy of *Goodbye Gordon Gekko* on his lap. I snapped a quick picture and sent it to all my friends under the caption: "Here's what Gordon Gekko thinks of my book."

■■■

As I looked out the window at 36,000 feet, my mind was racing. Although I am an optimistic person, I couldn't believe the transformation that had taken place in such a short time. In just one year, my company and I went from almost going out of business to hosting a wildly successful conference, appearing regularly on top business news networks, acquiring a fund of hedge funds business, having a cameo in an Oliver Stone blockbuster, and publishing a book. It was a lot . . . and we were trying to generate a return on our luck and good fortune.

And suddenly, amidst the clear blue, endless sky, I realized something—we were seemingly hopping over the rabbit hole. Rather than spiraling, twisting, and turning down an endless tunnel toward an illogical, nonsensical, and unknown demise, we were strategically taking control of SkyBridge's future by embracing our potential failures and turning them into potential successes.

It would have been easy to throw in the towel during those dark days and give up on the business, but that would have been selling out at the bottom. I take pride in the resilience our team showed and strive never to forget the tough times.

But even I must admit that I have never imagined the extent of my company's turnaround. Luck certainly had a hand in my good fortune. I can't deny that. But it came down to more than luck. I had stopped waiting for good things to happen. I had gone out and made them happen. Abraham Lincoln is credited with saying, "The best way to predict your future is to create it," and never before had I felt so in control of my own destiny. At least the parts I could control.

Chapter 2

From Peril to Pivot
Acknowledging Mistakes & Transitioning Ahead

"You don't learn by following rules. You learn by doing, and by falling over."

—*Sir Richard Branson*

The SALT Conference is the ultimate affirmation of my entrepreneurial beliefs. At a time when the financial system was collapsing and my business was failing, we took a bold risk to reinvigorate SkyBridge and positively shift the trajectory of the firm. We developed a different kind of conference, took on a different type of mind-set, and ultimately built a different type of business. Today, I carry that out-of-the-box approach into everything we do at SkyBridge.

The one constant in my career has been a burning desire to be an entrepreneur, to solve problems. In order to achieve that goal, I have been forced to embrace hardship. My career has been littered with failures, and my firm's success was ultimately defined by our ability to learn from mistakes and turn failures into success.

■■■

"We've got a big problem," Victor said on the other end of the phone.

"Have you ever heard of Deepavali?" he asked. "The Festival of Lights? It's is a holiday celebrated in Southeast Asia."

My throat tightened. Right away, I knew what he was about to say next. You see, my team and I had just come back from a month's worth of discovery meetings in Asia, where we met with prospective SALT delegates, speakers, and sponsors to raise awareness for the two-year-old SALT Asia Conference. And, something told me this holiday had something to do with our upcoming event.

He continued, "Well, the Monetary Authority of Singapore (MAS) called this evening to inform us that this holiday has now moved to Wednesday, October 22 . . . smack in the middle of our conference. Apparently, the date of this holiday moves each year due to the lunar calendar."

Before I could say a word, he continued, "And, they have asked that we consider moving the date or postponing SALT."

■■■

After the incredible success of SALT in Las Vegas, Victor and I decided to take the show on the road. Having seen the impact SALT had on our alternative asset business and brand awareness, we truly believed that we needed to expand beyond Vegas and the United States to help us create a truly global platform. In speaking with my partners, Asia seemed like the obvious choice, given our firm's—and the industry's—interest in raising capital from the region as well as in boasting allocations from Asia-based managers. If executed well, we believed that the conference could be a very effective tool for establishing bigger, broader relationships in the region. Once again, we were employing our Trojan Horse Strategy.

While Victor and I reached into our Rolodexes and sorted through old business cards to contact anyone we knew in Asia for their assistance, our team quickly got to work contacting the tourism boards for their assistance in helping us identify venues for the prospective event. We then impulsively booked the next flight to Hong Kong, where we proceeded to look at various skyscraping hotels throughout the magnificent city. From there, we traveled to Singapore and did the same. Something clicked for Victor and me while we were in the Jetson-like, sci-fi, futuristic city. Thanks to a booming private banking industry, the city was chock-full of ambitious visionaries who were seeking to take their companies to the next level. In a way, this entrepreneurial spirit was similar to the values we instilled at SkyBridge.

What's more, Singapore's flagship venue—the Marina Bay Sands Hotel, which was designed by famous Israeli architect Moshe Safdie and built at a staggering cost of $4.7 billion—was grand enough to host our projected 500-plus delegates. Boasting celebrity restaurants—such as Wolfgang Puck's legendary CUT restaurant—and an iconic rooftop pool that is considered to provide one of the "best views in the world," the Marina Bay Sands was in keeping with the image we sought to project to the world.

But, perhaps most importantly, we ultimately chose Singapore because of the government's willingness to endorse SALT and assist us throughout the planning process by providing key introductions to public policy officials and investors in the region.

Fast forward to October 2012. Thanks to the countless hours of our dedicated team—who literally worked both U.S. and Asia hours to pull this colossal event off—the inaugural SALT Asia Conference was a rousing success for SkyBridge, Singapore, and—perhaps, most significantly—for our delegates, speakers, and sponsors. The attendees raved about our distinguished list of accomplished keynotes, including former Vice President Al Gore, former British Prime Minister Tony Blair, and Michael Milken, while the media applauded our efforts in assembling 900 members of the global investment community together to facilitate discussions on the intersection of the global economy and the markets. What's more—SkyBridge started to build traction in the region, creating goodwill with Asian investors and allocators.

Given the rousing success of the conference—and industry feedback—we decided to sign a two-year contract with the Marina Bay Sands to host SALT Asia in September 2013 and October 2014. Based on the feedback of the delegates, the SALT Asia 2013 agenda focused more on financial and geopolitical discussions and featured Prime Minister Ehud Barak, Treasury Secretary Tim Geithner, Jean Claude Trichet, Jim Rogers, and more than 75 leading global investment managers. I also had the privilege of interviewing my dear friend—Wolfgang Puck, celebrity chef and serial entrepreneur—who then proceeded to prepare an intimate VIP dinner for me, my partners, and a select group of prospective SkyBridge clients and SALT speakers.

■■■

Fast forward to July 2014. We had already contracted the venue. We had secured our featured speaker—Ben Bernanke, who had just stepped down from the Fed—and were minutes away from signing two additional keynotes. We had created the website, sent invitations, and met with sponsors. We were far along in the discovery and planning process . . . just three months away!

"How did we miss this?" I asked Victor.

"Although it is no excuse, the observed holiday falls on a different day every year. And while it is being celebrated earlier in the week in other countries, Singapore will now be observing it on Wednesday." Victor sighed heavily. "I don't know what else to say . . . we messed up. Plain and simple."

As a side note—this was just one of many setbacks plaguing the 2014 Singapore conference. That same year, the government discontinued its nonstop flight from the States. Instead of a direct, 18-hour flight that made you miserable, now you were looking at a 27-hour trip that would leave you in full-blown tears. We believed this change would certainly restrict the number of North American participants.

"All right, we have to respect the suggestion of the Monetary Authority and postpone the event," I said to Victor. "That is an important relationship to the firm, one we must not jeopardize."

"And, we need to pivot," I continued. "We need to adapt. It is time to brainstorm."

With less than three months until SALT Asia, it was time to develop a new strategy.

The most common and biggest mistake many executives make is not admitting that they've made one. The hardest phrase for many entrepreneurs and CEOs to utter is, "I screwed up." Most would rather paint a rosy picture, either out of concern for losing their job or appearing weak to their employees. That's a big mistake. Admitting you're wrong is actually a sign of strong leadership. It demonstrates you have enough self-awareness and humility to take a step back, recognize what isn't working, and take the appropriate steps to fix it.

■ ■ ■

After assessing the entirety of the situation and consulting the necessary stakeholders, we devised a strategic, pivotal proposal that would satisfy the request of MAS and ensure that we fulfilled our previously confirmed commitments to our featured speakers, sponsors, and delegates, while minimizing our financial losses. But before we took any next steps—or made any public announcements—I told Victor that we must first speak to MAS as ensure that they were 100 percent on board with our decision. Upon a phone call to their senior team that evening, we collectively agreed to postpone the conference until further notice.

And, then the apology, tail-between-our-legs calls began. We called the Marina Bay Sands. Our confirmed speakers and sponsors. Our production partners. Our vendors. We drafted a statement—which MAS approved—and sent it to all of our media partners and—then—to all of our prospectively registered delegates.

By sunrise, we had put SALT Asia to bed. And before the bell was rung downtown at the New York Stock Exchange, we began working on the SkyBridge Global Symposium.

Remember, I told Victor we needed to pivot. Adapt. Brainstorm. The SkyBridge Global Symposium was our pivot. After all, we had contracts to fulfill, clients to serve, and vendors who relied on our paychecks for their livelihood. And, on a more applicable level, we had business to do and a reputation to maintain. You see, SkyBridge had recently gained substantial traction in potentially securing institutional mandates in Asia—and, particularly in Japan. What better way to strengthen these existing relationships—and identify and meet prospective investors—than by hosting an intimate, top-tier event where they had exclusive access to prominent thoughts leaders—like Dr. Ben Bernanke—and legendary hedge fund managers.

After a few long flights to Toyko—and, numerous late-night conference calls with our colleagues in Japan—we secured a venue, created a concise agenda and website, and curated a blue-chip list of 150 Asian investors who we knew were actively allocating to hedge funds. We hit the phones, proactively registering these investors while informing them about SkyBridge Capital.

In less than six weeks, we welcomed 120 institutional investors to the SkyBridge Global Symposium, where guests listened to an up-close-and-personal interview with Dr. Ben Bernanke, a SkyBridge Capital Overview presentation, and an interview with a hedge fund investment icon.

At the end of just one day, these existing and prospective clients walked away with a personal photo with Dr. Bernanke as well as first-hand knowledge about SkyBridge's core business, our product, and our offerings.

■■■

We turned what could have been an unmitigated disaster into a great opportunity for our firm, and we did it by following simple but very effective rules in our playbook.

Identify Mistakes & Acknowledge Errors

Dean Smith—legendary basketball coach at the University of North Carolina—once said, "What to do with a mistake: recognize it, admit it, learn from it, and forget it." Simply put—you will never be able to move forward and progress in your career if you are unwilling to identify your mistakes, put your ego on the floor, and admit your failures. Furthermore, intentionally hiding mistakes from your supervisors and trying to restore semblance and order without the consultation of your supervisors or partners only exasperates seemingly dire situations and leaves you and the team with few resources to rectify situations.

For example, in realizing the gravity of the problem, Victor did the right thing by informing me about of the situation. Sure, it might have seen easier for him to ignore the problem and continue to plan the conference, but that would have only compounded the immediate issue and potentially ruin our existing business relationship with the Singaporean government and regional investors.

Introspection, humility, transparency, and honesty are key ingredients to long-term success—both for the individual employee and for the betterment of the organization. Hubris and secrecy have no place in business.

On the other hand, it is important that managers provide safe, collaborative work environments where staff feel secure in admitting to a mistake or error. Having worked on Wall Street for over 30 years, I have never understood why certain organizations seek to elicit sheer fear of failure or misstep within their organizations. After all, another set of eyes is often invaluable in rectifying errors and improving dismal circumstances.

Pivot

After admitting a misstep, don't sulk, hide, or feel sorry for yourself. Don't continue to move forward because of your pride or ego . . . which will eventually ruin or destroy what you've been building as well as your brand. Instead, do whatever you can do to appropriately and ethically move on from the situation and then devise a strategic action plan to turn a potential disaster into a potential new venture and prosperous opportunity.

Okay, we made a mistake. Now what? You don't need to—and shouldn't want to—scrap everything. Instead, use your energy to pivot, design a transition plan and strategic execution strategy. While doing so, it's important to recognize the difference between a "sunk cost" and a "salvageable cost" as salvageable investments can often be incorporated into the new action plan. In the case illustrated on previous pages, the venue—the Marina Bay Sands—would be considered a "sunk cost" because we were unable to host the event in Singapore during the 2014 calendar year. On the other hand, the agreements that we had with our speakers, sponsors, and U.S.-based vendors would be considered a "salvageable cost" because we would utilize them while planning the SkyBridge Global Symposium.

In our situation, we looked for the best alternative and turned a potential disaster into an event that helped us grow our blossoming international institutional business.

Reflect and Learn

Mistakes and failures can be the most valuable resources for an entrepreneur.

Success glosses over weakness. Adversity exposes it and provides an opportunity to learn from it and work on it. When you do something right, there is a positive feedback loop that makes you feel invincible. When you do something wrong, you learn important lessons about yourself and the people around you. It's like a baseball team that plays with sloppy fundamentals on defense, but wins a stretch of games because of their ability to hit home runs. One day, the long ball will abandon you and the shoddy foundation will be exposed.

You should never regret making mistakes. Instead, value the lessons you learn from your inevitable failures. After all. If you're not making mistakes, you are probably not pushing yourself far enough.

Chapter 3

Fear. Failure. Focus.
Early Lessons in Entrepreneurship

"Nothing is more frustrating to an individualist than to be mired in a modern group-led, massive, corporate organization."

—Humphrey Neill

F rom a young age I knew I wanted to be an entrepreneur. Maybe I was inspired by my uncle's motorcycle shop, where I spent countless afternoons getting a first-class education in rolling up your sleeves and building a business. Maybe it was because I didn't like conforming to other people's schedules, and owning a company seemed to offer some measure of freedom. Either way, as far back as I can remember, all I really wanted to do was run my own company.

My first entrepreneurial venture was a smashing success. I was 12 years old. After being introduced to the *Long Island Newsday*'s incentive-based delivery program by childhood friend Paul Montoya—who is now the president of Media Sales at CBS Television—I built up the largest newspaper route in my hometown of Port Washington on Long Island, New York. To me, it wasn't really about selling newspapers and making money. Having extra cash in my pocket didn't hurt, but it was more about being the best—developing a reputation in the neighborhood of a hardworking, smart, reliable kid who was going to provide great customer service. I hustled my butt off selling papers to the Jewish, Italian, and Irish ladies in my neighborhood. To grow my route, every Wednesday I would ask my manager for a batch of free papers and go door-to-door in the apartment buildings handing them out. I kept meticulous notes on my red notepad, carefully documenting which apartments took the paper, and then the next day I'd go back to those same units in hopes of signing them up for a paid subscription.

"Did you enjoy your free paper?" I'd ask the nice ladies at the door, many of whom knew my mom. "Would you like to try a Sunday subscription? Maybe even daily? Do you like *Long Island Newsday*?"

There was no better feeling than converting one of these people into a first-time customer. I felt proud. Proud of my accomplishment. Proud that I was doing something that served people. Proud that I made people happy. Don't get me wrong . . . as a young kid from a middle-class household, I liked the money, too, and especially liked the tips. (Thank you, Mrs. Sheridan . . . She generously tipped 150%! To this day, I overtip like she did when I see hardworking people.) But more than anything, I loved the sense of pride I felt in building something. Of hustling day-in and day-out to earn my keep. Of being my own boss.

■ ■ ■

My second entrepreneurial venture did not turn out as well.

It was 1986. I was in my senior year at Tufts University. I wanted to go to Italy for a three-week post-graduation trip before starting Harvard Law in the fall; however, there was a small problem: I had no money. But thanks to my manager at the Espresso Pizza Shop, where I was working at the time, I came up with a plan to fund my trip.

"Hood Ice Cream Trucks," he told me. "I doubled my money in less than a weekend."

Hood Ice Cream was—and still is—a New England institution. The Massachusetts-based company has been around for more than 150 years and remains one of the country's largest dairy distributors. Part of their success is their short-term franchise model, in which motivated individuals can rent a truck and buy inventory to sell to consumers.

In any case, instead of asking follow-up questions about logistics and risks, I immediately took the $2,100 I had saved up from delivering newspapers and working various other odd jobs and rented a Hood Ice Cream Truck so I could sell iced confections during the Boston Marathon season. My plan was simple—I would double my money and rake in the sales from Marathon onlookers by setting up my truck along the race route.

Two days before the marathon, I filled up my Hood truck with Dove bars, frozen fruit bars, ice cream sandwiches, and drumsticks and drove down to Wellesley—the halfway point of the marathon on Route 16. I gave the manager of an Exxon station $50 to let me park on his property and use his electricity. With a few days to spare before the marathon, I drove around ringing the bell and selling ice cream while kids came running over, screaming their heads off. I was off to a good start . . . and it wasn't even race day. That's when I was going to make a killing . . . or so I thought.

On Marathon Monday, I drove the truck out to the Exxon station, plugged it in, and got ready to go . . . all the while fantasizing of Italian sunsets and coastline beaches. As I waited for spectators to start showing up, I could feel the rawness of an unusually cold and wet April day. Although average April temperatures were generally in the 50s, the temperature settled in the high 30s with nonstop rain.

As race fans ran for cover, I sat in my truck on the side of the road in disbelief. They say a good salesman can sell sand to a camel in the desert, but even my best pitch couldn't convince the few remaining spectators to buy an ice cream sandwich in 38-degree rain. I had no hedge. I had no cold-weather products to sell. No coffee. No hot chocolate. No donuts. Instead, I had a truck full of frozen confections that I couldn't return, as Hood's policy wouldn't allow me to take them back.

With all this inventory and no customers—and panicked not only about making it to Italy, but of breaking even—I drove around frantically to all the local delis trying to unload thousands of dollars' worth of unsold ice cream products before I had to return the truck.

At the end of the weekend, I was saddled with a $1,000 loss, money that had literally melted in the back of my truck. Instead of doubling my investment, I lost 50 percent.

■ ■ ■

The Hood Ice Cream Truck debacle would become the first of many painful failures in my career, but it offers five important lessons for entrepreneurs who want to avoid tumbling down the bottomless rabbit hole.

Stare Failure in the Face & Deal with It

Success should never be viewed as a given. If you are afraid of failure, don't become an entrepreneur. Success may not be something you can fully control. Having a great idea and working hard, while improving your odds, doesn't ensure success. Something entirely outside your control can set you back and knock you on your ass. That's failure, and you better be willing to embrace it if you're going to strike out on your own.

The sheer number of entrepreneurial success stories in America has created the false impression that being an entrepreneur is a can't-miss endeavor. It isn't. For every 23-year-old Silicon Valley billionaire, there are countless others who have failed miserably. Failure is always staring you in the face.

Operation Hood was an abject failure and an early lesson on the downside of entrepreneurship. But, as I mentioned in Chapter 2, you must transform your mistakes into valuable lessons. In this instance, my failure taught me that you should never invest all your money into one idea, and to always have a hedge in case your best-laid plans fail. I was so confident that I committed all my capital in the hopes of making a 100 percent return. I didn't and, as a result, lost money I couldn't afford to lose. Not only did I commit too much money to one idea, but I didn't even diversify my product offering. I had one product—ice cream—and it was virtually unsellable on a cold day.

Every business needs to have a diversified portfolio of ideas and products. If you're a one-trick pony, eventually you're going to be overrun by competitors. Diversify. There is an old aphorism that says put all your eggs in one basket and just watch the basket. There is some truth to that early on when you start a business, but even in the early stages you need to protect your downside.

The Hood Ice Cream Truck failure cost me my trip to Italy, but ultimately it was an inexpensive education in entrepreneurship. Sure, losing $1,000 hampered my ability to pay off a massive student loan debt, but it taught me not to be ashamed or deterred by failure. In fact, I took a certain pride in talking about it with my friends. My friends looked at me like I was an idiot. You know that look . . . the one that says, "Boy you are stupid, I would never let that happen to me." It's 30 years later and guess what? Very few of those people ever became entrepreneurs.

Don't Give Up

During your career—and in life—things will happen to you that are beyond your control. The market is going to crash for some unforeseen reason, or the seasoned person you just hired is going to suddenly leave the firm to pursue other opportunities. Stuff happens. What's really important is not what happens to you and your business but, rather, how you respond to what happens.

In the 9/11 attacks, Cantor Fitzgerald lost thousands of employees in the most horrific way possible. Closing up shop would have been a perfectly reasonable course of action. But in an act of American defiance and as a tribute to those lost, Howard Lutnick and the rest of the Cantor team simply refused to lie down. Today, the firm is stronger than ever.

There Is No Such Thing as a Free Lunch

However difficult you think starting a business will be, multiply that by 15 to get a realistic approximation. I don't care if it's selling ice cream or setting up a hedge fund; never expect entrepreneurship to be easy. It may well be rewarding, but it won't be easy.

In business, nothing worthwhile ever comes easy. What the media fails to tell you about overnight success stories is all the anxiety about meeting payroll and endless round-the-clock hours working on a project. The grind is constant.

The idea of starting from zero to build a large, sustainable business is incredibly daunting and intimidating. When I left the comfortable surroundings of Goldman Sachs to start my own business, I was terrified. Going out on my own made me self-conscious and filled me with self-doubt. Being consumed by the grand notion of "success" would have been overwhelming. Instead, I put my head down and got to work, focusing on closing every potential investor and unearthing one good investment idea at a time. The sum of those individual outcomes eventually added up to a robust business.

Simply put—if you aren't willing to put in the sweat equity, don't expect any equity.

Focus on Risk Relative to Reward

Every investment has potential return and inherent risk. In today's highly efficient and innovative marketplace, barriers to entry are high, and slam-dunk business ideas are few and far between. As an investor or entrepreneur, it is your job to seek the highest possible risk-adjusted returns.

Novice investors focus first and foremost on the potential pay-off while seasoned entrepreneurs pay more attention to the possible downside. That's not to say successful professionals are pessimistic—quite the contrary. But, savvy investors never put themselves in a position where their livelihood will be destroyed if something goes wrong. Aspiring business owners dream of the new BMW, the big house, and the private jet, while successful pioneers are motivated by the desire to build something and solve problems.

In the case of the Hood Ice Cream Truck, my eyes were open to the potential of doubling my money, but I should have been thinking about the very real possibility of significant losses. If selling ice cream products was always so easy, Hood would not contract with eager young people to purvey their goods and make sure there was no buy-back clause. The company is smart about passing along risk. Thank goodness I learned this lesson while I was young and the stakes were relatively low.

Focus on Process More than Outcome

Back to Dean Smith, the legendary college basketball coach who I introduced you to in Chapter 2 and who preached a philosophy of doing things the "right way," or focusing on the process of success rather than being fixated on the end result. In basketball that meant making the extra pass on offense, boxing out for rebounds, and moving your feet on defense. Over the course of a game, each individual play adds up to create the winning margin. Over the course of a season, those winning plays can help you grow into a champion. The idea is that if you focus on the process, on doing things the right way on a granular level, you will look up one day and be at your destination. Long-term goals are important to keep you driven and strategic, but your ability to execute on a day-in, day-out basis determines whether you succeed or not.

When I rented that ice cream truck, I was already dreaming of success, but my reality was failure. I had traveled in my mind to the moment I deposited the $5,000 cash in the bank and booked the flight to Italy. Meanwhile, I lost focus of the process. Attention to detail went out the window.

There are essential truths to becoming a successful entrepreneur. It requires hard work, sacrifice, strategic thinking, and risk-taking . . . to name a few. It also entails formulating an efficient process and a seamless execution strategy. But, perhaps more importantly, being an entrepreneur requires a level of acceptance. Things are never what they seem, especially when you start your own business. So, I'll state the golden rule again: If you are afraid of failure, don't become an entrepreneur. Rabbit holes are inevitable. Its how you hop over them that will define your success.

Chapter 4

Snap Out of It!
Looking Back to Move Forward

"For all sad words of tongue or pen,
The saddest of these: It might have been!"

—*John Greenleaf Whittier*

I f anyone tells you they have no regrets, look them in the eye, thank them for their time, and walk away. Why the complete disregard? Because they're lying. It's a simple fact of life: we all have regrets. If people are being truly honest with themselves, they will admit to having them. Some are mundane and insignificant, like "I should have worn those other shoes" or "I wish I'd ordered the filet instead of the veal." Some are more profound, like "I should have worked at a different company" or "I didn't go to the right school."

What regrets really speak to is a measure of self-awareness. The trick is how we choose to deal with them. Successful people have the ability to accept the past, embrace it, learn from it, and ultimately move forward. Less successful individuals tend to wallow in regrets, constantly reliving a series of events and asking themselves over and over what could have been, what should have been, and ultimately, what ought to have been. To me, there is no more dangerous word than *ought*. If you want to be happy and successful, remove it from your vocabulary. *Ought* conveys a sense of entitlement and prevents you from focusing on your future.

Things ought to be different.

I ought to have been made partner.

I ought to have been given a bigger bonus.

No, you shouldn't have. Whatever series of events conspired to separate what "ought" to have happened from what actually happened is ultimately your responsibility. Let me say that again. It is your responsibility. Deal with the world the way it is; not the way you want it to be or the way it ought to be. Own it.

When I was fired from Goldman Sachs, it wasn't because I was a wildly successful banker, or that I was making so much money for the firm, or because I was the smartest and most efficient worker. It wasn't because I had the best personality or that I was exceedingly pleasant to work with, either. At first, I tried to convince myself I was all of those things; that it was entirely someone else's fault, and that someone was out to get me.

When the initial anger subsided, I realized I got fired because I wasn't the right fit for the job. At first, I had difficulty embracing that reality. In my mind, I was canned because I was different, a middle-class kid from Long Island who didn't have the right connections or aptitude. They ought to have recognized just how smart I was. They ought to have known that I was an industrious and creative worker. Things ought to have worked out differently.

The reality was that I lacked the technical skills. I lacked the financial modeling skills. The job was a terrible fit for me, plain and simple. While it doesn't feel good to be forced to accept your own shortcomings, the experience sets the stage for a much better future. As much as anything, I proved to myself that I could get knocked down and get back up again. There's nothing like harsh reality to sober you up. I didn't have time for regrets. I had school debt . . . and plenty of it. Even if I felt paralyzed by regret, I had no choice but to snap out of it. I couldn't afford to wallow in self-pity. It was pure survival instincts that saved me from making perhaps the biggest mistake anyone can make: wallowing in self-pity.

Victimization, self-loathing, and self-pity are perhaps the most self-destructive behaviors a person can possess. They are incredibly addictive and powerfully destructive. They paralyze you and prevent you from taking action—any action—to change your course.

If you find yourself exhibiting these behaviors—and find yourself constantly reliving the past—my advice could not be simpler: STOP. Stop thinking about what could have been. It will not get you where you want to go. It will not change the past. Conversely, this preoccupation could actually alter the future. It will result in is making you miserable and incapable of making sound future decisions. After all, how can you begin to even think about the future if you are living in the past?

■ ■ ■

One of my biggest regrets wasn't something I did, but rather something I didn't do.

In my second go-round at Goldman Sachs, my job was selling research and products from the capital markets group—including Initial Public Offering (IPO) shares—to institutional customers. I was a much better salesman than I was an analyst. I knew how to listen, and I knew how to tell the company's and product's story.

One of my bosses was John P. McNulty, who would later become head of Goldman's Investment Management Division and a member of the Management Committee. To this day, John remains one of the most gifted people I've ever met. He was strategic and had incredible people skills. He was generous with his time and cared about employees and putting people in a position to succeed. He promoted scores of people through the ranks at Goldman, and was just an overall classy guy with a very warm, inviting smile.

I remember my first major encounter with John. It came during preparations for the CBL Associates IPO. CBL Associates—one of the largest mall operators in the United States—represented a revolutionary approach to retail. The company brought the urban retail experience to suburban shopping malls in the southeastern United States, making a fortune in the process.

CBL's CEO was a man named Charles Lebovitz. His father had run a series of drive-in movie theaters across the South. Sensing that the days of drive-ins were numbered, Charles converted those movie theaters into shopping malls. It was a brilliant pivot that capitalized on changing consumer preferences and behavior. People weren't going to drive-in movies anymore, but they *were* spending more and more time in their cars. They were doing different things, like driving to the mall. It may seem obvious now, but at the time, it was an out-of-the-box approach to hopping over the rabbit hole by pivoting a business. It represented a quantum leap in retail strategy.

In any case, CBL was preparing for what was expected to be a huge IPO, and Charles—along with a group of his top executives and about 15 to 20 Goldman bankers—were crowded into the Goldman Partners Amphitheater on the 30th floor at 85 Broad Street. Charles was standing on the podium going through a dry run of next week's road show, the event where we would market CBL shares to various institutions and investors. Charles had a very inviting, professorial face, and he wore exquisitely tailored, understated custom suits. Despite speaking with a very deliberate cadence, he always seemed like a guy exceedingly comfortable in his own skin. But for whatever reason, when he went up to the podium that day he seemed stiff, robotic, and overrehearsed.

He kept repeating the talking points the bankers had prepared for him: Earnings before interest, return on equity, price to sales, sales per square foot, and so on. On and on he went, putting everyone in the audience into a deep, restful sleep. It was brutal. The spiel was more effective than any sleeping pill on the market. However, the bankers in the front row apparently loved it. When he finally finished—having exhausted every mundane statistic known to man—the reaction in the room would have made you think the man had just hit a walk-off home run in game seven of the World Series. Everyone couldn't stop clapping.

"Excellent!" they said.

"Really strong, Charles. You totally nailed it," another banker chimed in.

Charles let a nervous smile take over his face.

"With all due respect, sir, I thought it was horrible." I bellowed from just a couple rows behind the sycophant bankers.

You could feel the sphincters in the front row tighten all at once. Their heads swiveled in unison to look back at me with an expression of shock, confusion, rage, and fear. In their minds, the outburst only reinforced the reason why I was originally fired. I had just violated the obsequious clause in Goldman's client protocol handbook. Or had I?

Charles shot me a puzzled look, but he didn't seem angry. He seemed curious.

"What did you not like about it?" Charles asked, politely.

"Look," I respectfully said. "You have this amazing story. You're the Sam Walton of commercial real estate."

As I spoke, I could see the corners of his mouth start to lift.

"You went outside the urban markets that were super-dense in population and you created these shopping malls in suburban and rural areas where there was no competition, and you got people to drive 20 minutes to come to these malls. You also put great seating and entertainment in the common areas so people could not only shop but they could spend the day there. That was Sam Walton's strategy for beating Sears. You've got to tell that story. That's your story. You've got to talk about how that idea came to you and how you created this incredible business that has literally changed people's lives. The talking points are fine; you can weave them into narrative. But they can't *be* the narrative. If you tell the story behind the idea, people are going to love it."

Stunned silence . . .

To his credit, Charles wasn't offended by anything I said. In fact, it was just the opposite. He was intrigued. He walked over to me, past his cadre of advisers and lieutenants, past the suits, and sat down right next to me a couple rows back.

"Would you lend me your pen?" he asked. "I want to take notes. Tell me more."

I told him his own amazing story, how he wasn't just an operator and developer of strip malls, but rather a visionary entrepreneur whose company was changing the way people lived. He was opening up new markets and helping companies like Gap and The Limited grow their sales.

"Tell that story," I implored. "And *then* work in all that other stuff."

Still, the room was dead silent, waiting for Charles to speak again.

"I like it. Let's do that."

Later that night, after everyone had gone home, John McNulty called me into his office.

"You have a real set of balls on you," he told me, reaching across his desk to shake my hand and flashing a wide, amused smile. "When you told Charles his presentation sucked—I've got to tell you, I wanted to whack you in the head. But it worked. He loves you. Nice going."

"I had to get his attention," I replied, sheepishly. "He wouldn't have gotten the message if I told him what he wanted to hear . . . like everyone else. I had to give it to him bluntly in order to get him to start thinking about his company differently."

I'll admit it: telling Charles his presentation sucked was an enormous risk. He could have gotten pissed, kicked me out of the room, and fired me on the spot.

Most managers would have. Most managers don't want a loose cannon on their team. They want capable robots. But not John. He was different. He wanted people who were willing to take calculated risks, who weren't afraid to lay it on the line. He knew how to let people grow and be productive in the context of a team. I had the opportunity to stay and keep working for John in one of the fastest-growing units at one of the greatest investment banks of all time. I could have had a front-row seat to greatness and work for one of the most gifted businesspeople I'd ever met. John was a fantastic mentor to me. I could have worked for him for three or four more years and become a much more seasoned executive.

■ ■ ■

Emboldened by my unending drive and desire to be an entrepreneur, I soon set out to start my own business. Raw entrepreneurial ambition blinded me to the opportunities that were right in front of my face. I had—and continue to have—a desire to create something from nothing.

And there you have it. One of my biggest regrets in life is not working for John longer . . . Truth be told, had I continued to work for John, I'd probably be right where I am today but would have had a smoother journey. John would have helped me remove that large chip on my shoulder sooner and taught me how to not take everything so personally. He would have taught me many of the lessons I eventually learned the hard way . . . many of which I will vulnerably share with you throughout this book.

That said, there is always a silver lining to all events that take place in your life—good or bad. Leaving Goldman to start my own business has taught me the importance of not taking situations for granted. It taught me about the importance of putting long-term goals ahead of short-term ambitions, something I try to remember in my day-to-day approach to life.

Unfortunately, John had his life taken way too early and passed away of heart disease in 2005. Former Goldman Sachs CEO Hank Paulson—who served as President George W. Bush's Treasury secretary during the 2008 financial crisis—told me last year he often wished he had John's sage counsel during those dark days in Washington, D.C. John McNulty is still missed.

Chapter 5

An Entrepreneurial Blueprint

The Don'ts of Building a Business

"It's not the strongest of the species that survive, nor the most intelligent, but the one most responsive to change."

—Charles Darwin

t was January 2004. I was a managing director at Lehman Brothers. And it was comp day.

"Your base pay is $400,000. We're also giving you a $700,000 bonus—$600,000 is your firm bonus; $100,000 is the team bonus that's granted to you as several managing directors believe that you're a team player. So your total compensation for your efforts at Lehman Brothers is $1.1 million."

"Thank you," I said, respectfully.

"You seem upset," he paused. "Do you think you were unfairly compensated?"

"I didn't say that," I said as I stood up. "I simply said 'thank you.'" I shook his hand and left the conference room.

By any stretch of the imagination, $1.1 million was—and still is—a tremendous sum of money to make in one year. Growing up on Long Island in the 1970s, I would never have dreamed of reaching that level of annual income. However, in the bank account–measuring contest on Wall Street, I was being compensated as a middling, journeyman managing director at Lehman Brothers. Although the compensation might have been deserved at the time, that characterization didn't sit well with me.

I sold my first company, Oscar Capital, to Neuberger Berman in 2001. Just two years later, Neuberger merged with Lehman Brothers, who effectively became my employer. Within a few months, I asked the newly established management for a broader portfolio of responsibility; however, my request was never responded to or acted upon. Apparently, you needed to bleed team green, have grown up in the company's culture, and learned how to answer directives with a set of programmed responses in order to be embraced by the Lehman Brothers management.

Although this is not meant to be a disparagement, I—and many others—found the culture of Lehman Brothers to be political, insular, and—at times—toxic. In fact, they required all managing directors to take a Myers-Briggs personality test so that they could measure your results against Dick Fuld's test results and how well your personality matched your MD peer group's results. The bad news for me was that I failed on both accounts—I scored completely opposite from Mr. Fuld *and* my results indicated that my personality matched less than 4 percent of my colleagues. What's more, I received these results from a rather passive-aggressive human resources director who said in pitch-perfect Lehman-speak, "This test is very telling. Perhaps this firm really isn't the right fit for you."

That was the beginning of the end. I knew the results would lead to an inevitable confrontation that had been bubbling under the surface.

Again, I don't mean to scorn Lehman Brothers, but the story is a cautionary tale about working in organizations that have "group-think" and "yes man" cultures. When you create a highly competitive, bureaucratic, and politicized work environment—where every employee acts solely out of self-interest and self-preservation—the slope toward implosion becomes very slippery. Windows get broken, dishonesty and paranoia run rampant, and accountability and loyalty fall by the wayside. And, the next thing you know, the culture has descended so far into the abyss that many talented, hardworking, and innovative people can no longer save it. It isn't obvious, but it happens in a way that no one ever expects.

In any case, I cashed that final bonus check and submitted a formal resignation to the firm, targeting Friday, March 4, 2005, as my last day. There wasn't a lot of ceremony upon my departure, just stacks of paperwork.

■ ■ ■

On Monday, March 7, 2005, I founded SkyBridge Capital. Despite working on Wall Street—a fraternity obsessed with status and titles—I knew that I never wanted to be a cog in an already established machine. I wanted to build something. I dreamed as a kid about running my own business and couldn't live with myself if I didn't try. So off I went again, leaving to start a new company. The overall premise was the same: Build a great product, care about servicing my clients, and grow my business. I was stepping out of my core circle of competence, but I figured hedge fund seeding couldn't be too hard. A combination of ignorance and audacity fueled my dream.

The original mission of the firm was a somewhat novel approach to the hedge fund seeding business. A traditional hedge fund seeder invests money in promising start-up hedge funds to help them get their feet off the ground. In the seeding business, you're basically trying to discover the talented managers of tomorrow, in much the same way that an agent might scout a baseball prospect.

In the early days of the firm's existence, I was flooded with fear, self-doubt, and anxiety. The uncertainty didn't help me sleep at night. I was 41. I'd already had one successful business, but was I really prepared to start something out of nothing all over again? I was confident we were filling a need in the marketplace, but we didn't have a tried-and-true business model. We had no assets under management and no operational personnel. Our global headquarters was slightly larger than three Dilbert cubicles, which we rented at a month-to-month hedge fund hotel.

During those stressful early days, the skepticism wasn't just internal. I got calls from several of my former colleagues at Lehman questioning how I was going to make such a dramatic career move. My prior experience did not necessarily qualify me as an asset manager, so how was I going to build a hedge fund seeding business? Former colleagues bluntly told me, "You shouldn't be doing this. . . . You're already in your 40s and considered a middle-aged sales guy on Wall Street. . . ." In other words, you don't have the reputation to pull it off.

A friend of mine from Goldman Sachs, whose words, frankly, carried a little more weight, said plainly, "You're not going to make it. This is a tough business and only seasoned guys who understand the hedge fund business are capable of doing this sort of thing."

While not exactly brimming with confidence at this point, I continued to forge ahead. After giving my first public presentation on the new company, a family office executive agreed to meet me in the Starbucks at the Sony atrium in Midtown Manhattan. "Okay, this is a start; I'll take it," I said to myself. But instead of wanting to give me money, he insisted on buying me a cup of coffee and giving me a lecture.

"Listen, this product has no track record. You're asking for a three-year lockup, you're asking for fees on uncommitted capital, and no one knows what hedge fund managers you're actually going to invest in. Not even a combo of Harry Houdini, the Easter Bunny, and Santa Claus could raise this money. Quit now and go look for a job before you ruin your reputation."

At least I had some honest friends!

The most stinging inquisition, though, came from my sweet, innocent, nine-year-old daughter, Amelia, who said, "Dad, don't you work at Lehman Brothers?"

"I used to."

"Isn't Lehman Brothers a very big company?"

"Yes, sweetheart."

"Well, what is SkyBridge? It seems like just an idea you scribbled down on a piece of paper. Lots of my friends' dads work at banks like Lehman Brothers, and no one has ever has heard of SkyBridge. Why would you leave Lehman Brothers to work at a made-up company like SkyBridge?"

It's no wonder that Amelia is now flourishing as a professional performer and young adult 11 years later. In those few sentences, she got to the core of what entrepreneurs are up against. Going from nowhere to somewhere always feels like an arduous—even impossible—dream . . . especially in the beginning.

■■■

When most people think of hedge funds, they think of sleek offices lined with premium materials and expensive art. Our first setting couldn't have been farther from that vision. We literally subletted three office cubicles from our prime broker and settled in a small space located at 527 Madison Avenue. Our office was like a tree house stuck inside a Manhattan office building, with nondescript gray tables and walls under white fluorescent lights. There were three of us with six screens, six phones, and one fax machine. Everything we used to run the business was on a month-to-month lease. And we had zero clients.

At Lehman, I was in a client relationship role. I was not a traditional money manager who could take his clients with him. All I really had was a business concept called SK Capital. My idea was simple: I wanted to combine a traditional hedge fund seeding business with a powerful sales and marketing force that could help raise large amounts of capital. We would give promising new funds money to grow and scale their business and strategies. Not only would our customers participate in the profits of the funds, but they would also own small pieces of the firms.

Some of the most successful hedge funds have been seeded in this way. Take Och-Ziff Capital, for example. Today, it has more than $30 billion in assets under management, but the company was started back in 1994 when the billionaire Ziff brothers gave Goldman Sachs's rising star Danny Och $100 million to start his fund. Similarly, Sam Wyly dipped into his billions and seeded Lee Ainslie so that he may start his own fund, Maverick Capital, in 1993. It went on to become one of the most successful hedge funds of all time. The list goes on and on. In any case, the seeding business had a precedent for success, and I believed we had a chance to create something special.

My pitch was simple: a lot of hedge funds use the words *limited* and *partnership* together, but they tend to place too little emphasis on finding truly good partners. In fact, the word *limited* always seemed more important than the word *partner* in the relationship. As such, we set out to create value for the funds while putting our investors in the general partner's position, allowing them to share in the fees.

While our pitch was solid, our name, SK Capital—an abbreviation of Scaramucci and the last name of my former partner, Andy Klein— was not. It just never seemed to roll off the tongue. We needed a better name. Something more memorable. And one day, it hit me on my drive into the city.

"Help me find a name that rhymes with Highbridge," I asked my colleague over the phone.

A couple of months earlier, JPMorgan had bought a controlling interest in Glenn Dubin's Highbridge Capital for reportedly over a billion dollars. At the time, I thought it would be good karma for us if we could somehow rename our firm with something that rhymed with Highbridge, as this was one the largest hedge fund acquisitions ever. As soon as I got into the office, my small team and I started googling names, starting with A, moving to B and C, and so forth. Finally, we got to S.

"SkyBridge is not taken, and with the S and the K we can kind of retain the SK but rename ourselves SkyBridge."

So, five months after starting SK Capital, we made the first of what would become many hops over the rabbit hole, renaming ourselves "SkyBridge Capital."

■ ■ ■

Starting your own business is the most terrifying and nausea-inducing thing you can do. It will cause you to lose sleep and—in the beginning—money that you don't have. It will cause you to obsessively eat, incessantly stress, gain weight, and perhaps develop an ulcer or two if you're doing it right. (All the stress of starting SkyBridge led me to develop a habit of grinding my teeth while sleeping, which forced me to wear a Lucite mouth guard).

But when it all comes together, you gain something else. Something greater than pride. Something money can't buy. Any entrepreneur knows the feeling but can't fully describe it. For me, it was the moment when I walked into my office, turned the lights on, and looked around and said to myself, "This is our company. And, it's a real company with real people actually working at it and—perhaps more importantly—relying on its success to support them and their families." It was at that moment when I left like I was doing exactly what I was put on Earth to do.

■ ■ ■

While the feeling of making the entrepreneurial breakthrough feels supernatural, the path to success is distinctly human. For every entrepreneur who succeeds, there are handfuls of those who don't. The odds are hard and the deck is often stacked against you, but there are certain things you can do to give yourself a better chance of reaching your goals.

If you're starting a new business, it's not enough to have a great product or business. You need to avoid the following four common mistakes that most entrepreneurs make.

Don't Spend Money on the Wrong Things

A long-time private client of mine—who happened to be on the Goldman Sachs Management Committee—asked if I would meet with a potential partner of his who had just started his own investment shop. It was the mid-1990s and I was running Oscar Capital.

"He's extremely smart," my friend told me over the phone. "You're going to love this guy. When he was at Goldman, he was one of our top bond traders. Let me know what you think of him. I'm thinking of giving him some money."

I welcomed the opportunity, as I always felt confident in my ability to make judgments on people fairly quickly. And who knows, maybe I'd invest some money with him, too.

"Anthony, so great to meet you," he said when I entered his office.

His hair was perfect. His custom Loro Piana suit and Hermes tie were exquisite. The guy looked like a male model. But what really blew me away was his office.

Although his office was located in an old, ordinary, nondescript building with an unremarkable lobby on Wall Street, his office floor was a site out of an *Architectural Digest*. Apparently, he had recently done a gut renovation and had imported premium materials, hired the best designers, and spared no expense on the interior décor. To this day I have never seen a more impressive office. Natural lighting perfectly kissed the surface of the imported Italian marble and beautiful oak wood carvings on the wall.

"This is some office you have here," I said to him. You would have thought I just paid him the highest compliment in the world.

"Thanks," he replied, beaming. "Let me give you the VIP tour."

For the next 40 minutes he led me through each room, talking about this custom chair and that rare fabric. We stopped every so often to marvel at his fine art collection, which was scattered throughout the space.

"This piece was actually on loan at the Tate," he proudly offered.

When we finally settled into sleek Barcelona chairs in his office, we talked business. At this point, I was actually dizzy from all the talk of textiles and impressionism, but he provided some real insights and original ideas on fixed income markets. He was an extremely knowledgeable and skilled investor, which I guess wasn't a big surprise considering he was a former managing director of fixed income at Goldman—a position you don't attain by being a dummy.

I sat. I listened. I thanked him for his time. And when I returned to the Oscar offices, the contrast couldn't have been anymore stark. I immediately called my friend who made the referral.

"Nice guy. Smart guy," I said into the phone. "Too bad he'll be out of business in a year."

"What are you talking about?" My friend shot back. "He's a brilliant bond trader."

"He may be world's best bond trader," I said, "but he has no idea how to run a business."

I was wrong . . . he was out of business in *two* years. The second I stepped into his plush palace, I knew he was toast. That's because he had just committed one of the biggest cardinal sins as an entrepreneur: overspending on the wrong things. Too much marble and oak. Focusing on sizzle—rather than substance—causes businesses to fail. There was an embedded arrogance in that approach, a lack of understanding that to really run a business you have to be mindful of costs and send a message to staff about thriftiness.

Contrast that with legendary hedge fund investor David Tepper. His pragmatic approach to investing mirrors his approach to business. The first time I walked into his nondescript New Jersey office, there was only one thing for me to look at: his ideas. He didn't waste a half hour giving me a lecture on modern art or telling me about his new boat. He got right down to business. He wasn't there to waste anybody's time. This humble approach helped him build Appaloosa Management into one of the greatest hedge funds of all time.

This is an important lesson for any entrepreneur—if you are starting a new business, you should maintain the appearance of a start-up. You want people to know that you are hungry and focused on one thing: work. Your customers come first. Your employees come a close second. The art comes at the very, very end . . . if at all. Spend the money on things that matter. Always keep your expenses down.

Don't Think You Can Do It Alone

Given my lecture about the perils of excessive overhead this may strike you as ironic, but another common mistake people make when starting a business is not hiring enough people. In a world of increasing automation, people are still the most important part of most businesses. People come up with ideas. People build lasting relationships. People are creative. Staffing is also the most efficient way to give your business the aura of survivability. While authenticity always trumps perception, it's important to project a sense that your business is thriving. And, a team of talented employees sends that message.

The average new business fails within five years. In the very beginning, you cannot usually hire a group of people and pay them all a ton of money without establishing the viability of your business model. But, you need to hire like-minded, driven people who believe in the vision of the company and complement your skill-set. Making sure you put the right people in place is one of the most important things you can do when you're starting a business.

Don't Overcomplicate Your Idea

I turned on the tap and a brown liquid poured out. I jumped back from the sink.

"What the heck is that?" I asked my roommate.

It was 1985. I was taking a semester abroad at the London School of Economics. I was living in Norfolk Square at a hotel where students were housed. The accommodations were more hostel than hotel, but I didn't really care. I wasn't there to be inside all day anyway, and it served my needs just fine. But the lack of clean water was, let's say, less than ideal.

I called down to building management and he reassured me in a thick British accent that despite the brownish tint, the water was "very safe indeed, sir" for consumption. "I drink it every day," he told me.

I wasn't a finicky guy. My mother used to take an empty glass milk bottle, wash it, fill it up with tap water, and put it in the fridge. That was our bottled water, and I never thought for a second that it could harm me (and it never did). But there was no way I was going to drink that brown stuff.

I wandered out to the local market and purchased my first bottled water. It was Evian, to be exact. At first, I thought the whole concept was a joke. The only people I saw openly consuming bottled water were health freaks and yuppies. I didn't really fit into either crowd. That said, it sure did beat the brown sludge coming out of my faucet so my roommate and I splurged on a couple bottles of Evian at two pounds apiece. It was a lot of money back then, not to mention the fact we were spending it on the Earth's most abundant natural resource.

Little did I know the bottled water industry was about to go on an uninterrupted bull market for the next three decades. Americans now drink more bottled water than milk or beer. In 1976, the average American drank a gallon and a half of bottled water every year. By 2012, that number jumped to almost 31 gallons annually. And, I must admit, I myself have never kicked the habit and still drink Evian to this day.

The more I thought about Evian, the more it demonstrated one of the most important rules for any entrepreneur—the simplest ideas are usually the best. How often are you taken aback by the sheer brilliance and simplicity of an idea? It usually involves an aspect of something that currently exists in your life, just packaged and sold to you differently.

■ ■ ■

Simplicity has always been the lifeblood of entrepreneurs. If you're look-ing for the next great idea, perhaps you are looking too hard. Perhaps the next great invention is right in front of your eyes. Most great entre-preneurs are less Einstein and more MacGyver, skilled at improvisa-tion and seeing the world through a creative lens. Take Howard Schultz, founder & CEO of Starbucks, for example, who essentially repackaged something so familiar—coffee—into a $100 billion business and turned a painstakingly simple idea into a cultural phenomenon. Having traveled to Milan, he claimed he had an "epiphany" while sitting in one of the many coffee shops. He saw firsthand the role a local espresso bar can have on the culture and social life of a city. It can be the center of a neighborhood, the lifeblood of a village, or a place where people meet, linger, and pass the day.

As a result of this experience, Schultz created Starbucks—adapting his Italian experience to American tastes. Instead of an open cafe, Schultz offered sandstone floors; comfortable furniture; wireless Internet; consistently good drinks; and quick, friendly, reliable ser-vice. Fast-forward to today, and there are close to 12,000 Starbucks in the United States (and that doesn't include the many Starbucks over-seas). It seems that people can't get through the day without a cup of Starbucks. People don't mind paying extra money for this daily fix as it is a positive, convenient, and consistent experience.

You don't have to be brilliant to be a successful entrepreneur. Let me rephrase that—you don't have to fit the classical definition of genius in order to build a successful business and have a huge impact on the world. You just need a brilliantly simple idea that you can exe-cute consistently.

Don't Reinvent the Wheel

Most great companies and entrepreneurs don't reinvent the wheel. They simply adapt and improve it.

Take Virgin Airlines, for example. They have reinvented the modern-day commercial airline experience through their commitment to the customer experience and sleek design. Commercial airline travel today is tantamount to torture, but it wasn't always like that. In the 1950s and 1960s, flying was a glamorous event that people actually got dressed up for. The planes served good food, poured strong drinks, and offered friendly service. Flying was an all-around pleasant experience. Fast-forward to today, where seats are small, attendants aren't attentive, meals are no longer served, and passengers are sometimes unruly. . . . Unless you are flying Virgin Airlines. They were the first airline to restore glamour to air travel . . . and, thankfully, the other airlines have followed suit and have made vast improvements. Through their sleek interior cabin designs, in-flight cart-free snack service, modern plane safety videos, and friendly customer service, they have made flying somewhat pleasurable again. What's more—they pioneered the concept of the fully reclined, plush seat. For years, travelers never had the ability to fully recline and lie flat in the seat. The plane simply didn't have enough space, but Virgin shifted the angle of their seats 30 degrees, and in doing so configured their cabins in such a way that one could recline all the way, and in the process, make a bed in the sky.

Similarly, Steve Jobs didn't invent the cell phone—he reinvented it. He made it cool and intuitive. People may forget just how clunky mobile phones used to be, and I'm not talking about those bricks people used to lug around in the 1980s. I'm talking about the awkward flip phones that were ubiquitous just 10 years ago. You couldn't play music on them. You could barely take a photo, let alone a video. Surfing the Web? Don't even think about it. The iPhone changed all that. It allowed people to have all their devices—camera, phone, music, video, e-mail—in one simple and sleek device. The browser was a revelation. Even if you weren't a techie, you still had to have it. It was empowering as an information access tool and as a small computer. (I have even typed out several passages of this book using Google Docs on my iPhone.) The iPhone simplified the mobile computing experience and created whole new industries, but at its heart, it's still a phone.

In the same way Virgin and Apple reimagined existing commodities, we tried to put our own unique spin on the SALT Conference.

Putting on the same old stale type of conference wasn't enough; we wanted to create something fresh. As mentioned previously, our goal was not to make money off the actual conference but to use it as an opportunity to build our brand and develop relationships. For that reason, we carefully curated the delegate list, ensuring that the vast majority of attendees would be investors and asset allocators, while the vast minority would be service and data providers, lawyers, and accountants. This delegate composition was a counterintuitive approach to the conference business.

In the end, we wanted to be the *Tonight* show, the *Today* show, and the *60 Minutes* of the conference industry. We wanted to be to the conference industry what *Monday Night Football* was to sports—an institution. As we plan the conference every year, we think of ways to freshen it up. We never want SALT to fall down the rabbit hole, to become tired and contrived. We ask ourselves, "What do people want this year?" What people wanted in 2009 is not going to work in 2017. We reinvent ourselves every year. We always evolve, as the world and business are always changing.

We're not Apple or Starbucks—I would never put myself in the same universe as Steve Jobs or Howard Schultz—but we try to emulate their entrepreneurial acumen at SkyBridge Capital and with the SALT Conference. Take the mundane, and reimagine it with more ambition and creativity. It's often the simple, yet powerful, ideas that can be the biggest—and, the most game-changing—ideas.

Chapter 6

Holding Grudges
Brush that Chip Off Your Shoulder

"Discipline, which is but mutual trust and confidence, is the key to all success in peace and war."

—General George S. Patton Jr.

On the cab ride down to the West Village, I kept replaying what my boss had told me earlier in the day in my head. "Come on over to my apartment. I want to have a private conversation with you." Mike Fascitelli wasn't just my boss. He was also my friend and mentor in the real estate division of Goldman Sachs's investment bank. Though he wasn't a partner yet, he was clearly on his way to big things at the firm. He was someone people liked and wanted to work hard for—a true leader.

Still, I had a knot in my stomach. Fascitelli wanted me to go to his Jane Street apartment . . . not meet in the office . . . for a private conversation. . . . What exactly did that mean? I continued to dissect his words, but it didn't take a genius to figure out what was on his mind.

It was 1991. The real estate market was struggling. Just looking out the window of the cab, you could see a city languishing in a recession.

Vacant lots sat where gleaming towers were supposed to rise. Empty storefronts were everywhere.

"Come on in. Have a beer," Mike said as I entered his apartment. Mike was 35 at the time. He was fit, with a thick head of dark hair and piercing eyes. He must have worked 15-hour days, yet he kept in good shape and was an energetic guy.

"Okay," he said as the Chicago Bulls game played in the background. "I'll get to the point. We're letting go of about 35 people—about a third of the group, ranging from associates to vice presidents—and you are one of them."

Unlike a lot of managers, Mike was always direct and honest. He didn't mince words or make you suffer in awkward silence.

We didn't break eye contact the entire time. I was numb. His words just lingered. I heard what he said but didn't fully process what he was saying.

Before I had a chance to ask why, the straight talk continued.

"I could probably keep you," Mike added, "but I think it's best that you go. I don't think you are particularly good at what you do, and it would be better for you and the firm if you left and found a position that's a better fit for you and your skill set."

I couldn't really think of anything to say. He was right, but I could tell Mike wasn't taking pleasure in delivering the message. He gave me the news in much the same way a doctor might tell his patient that he's terminally ill. He might as well have been telling me I was dying, too. His tone was steady and calm the entire time.

"You don't have the technical skills for this job. We hired you because we liked your personality and work ethic and thought we could train you, but the truth of the matter is in the current climate, the firm does not want to take the time to go through that training. Keeping you around would not be in your best interest."

"Wow!" I thought to myself. "It was all so brutally honest." I was starting to regain my bearings. "Okay," I thought, "let's just recap this. I am not the right fit for this job. You could save me if you wanted to, but you clearly don't think I'm a worthwhile investment. Holy crap . . . I just got fired."

The shock turned to anger.

"Did you just fire me?" I screamed inside my head. "Stay cool," I reminded myself. But the words were starting to come out anyway.

"I can't believe you are doing this to me," I said to him, hoping my voice wouldn't crack. I swallowed deeply, trying to regain my composure. I could feel my heart rate increasing. "I just cannot believe you are doing this to me," I said again. The enormous chip I had lugged on my shoulder from childhood was growing heavier by the second. Coming from a middle-class Italian American family on Long Island, you were always fighting for people to take you seriously. When someone slighted you, you remembered it. Embarrassment and shame were the worst feelings of all. It was an infantile approach—one I thought I'd left behind in college—but it was all coming back to me in a torrent of anger and resentment.

"Listen," Mike said, momentarily distracting me from my inner temper tantrum. "I used to be a consultant at McKinsey. You're going through SARAH," he said.

I shot him a look like he was speaking Chinese. "Who the hell is Sarah?"

"Sarah. S-A-R-A-H," Mike calmly said to me. "Shock. Anger. Rejection. Acceptance. Help," Mike said with emphasis. "This is what happens when something traumatic happens, and right now you're probably in shock," he added. "You will move quickly into anger, but listen to me." He paused to make sure I was looking him in the eye. "This is important, Anthony. You've got to move through that stuff. And you've got to accept this is happening to you."

My heart slowed a little. "Life is unfair," he added for good measure. "But, I know you will find the right job for you and do great things in life."

I stood up, shook his hand, and headed for the door. My impulse was to lash out, but I am very grateful that I didn't. If you are ever fired from a job, handle it with grace, dignity, and kindness. Nothing good will come from being bitter and angry. If you talk through it rationally, you will both keep your reputation intact and learn about your shortcomings.

Granted, in the moment, it's not so easy to have perspective.

On the way back home from Mike's apartment my head was spinning. Then the panic began to set in. Oh my God. I went to Harvard Law School. I owe thousands of dollars in student loan debt, and I just got fired from Goldman Sachs. My fancy degrees felt more like marks of shame than accomplishments. I decided to work at Goldman because it was the most prestigious firm that paid the most money. And, now I had to face the world—and my mother—and tell them I was fired.

I got back to my little apartment above a bowling trophy shop in Tarrytown, New York. Maybe it would be best to get some sleep, something I had been deprived of during my stint at Goldman. But when I woke the next morning, the wounds were still raw. I went on an extra-long run to clear my mind. The air was freezing and burning my lungs, but it helped me wake up to my current situation. At 27, I was still relatively young. Whatever career I had in front of me, I knew I at least had the benefit of time. I thought back to Mike's stages of grief, his SARAH. Maybe I could get through the S, the A, and the R, but the acceptance would take some time.

■ ■ ■

Of course, I took the firing very personally. People will tell you "business isn't personal," but I've always found it hard to separate the two. If you don't take pride in what you do and if you don't set a personal standard for everything you do, you should probably do something else. The message behind the cliché makes a little more sense, I guess. You can't let business decisions lead to personal vendettas. Resentment and grudges are unhealthy and simply waste time. You have to find a way to remove that chip from your shoulder.

Revenge is attractive in theory, but is almost always unfulfilling. In fact, it's often the contrary. Revenge hurts those seeking it the most. When something goes against you at work, you basically have two choices: leave the company or figure out a way to make it work. While you may be justified in your anger and you may have been treated unfairly, life doesn't keep score. What you ultimately seek is respect and acknowledgment for your hard work, which will come only if you have the discipline to make well-reasoned decisions.

If you choose to stay within an organization, you have to be a part of a collective effort. Think about some of the greatest leaders in history. Many of them worked with their one-time adversaries. Winston Churchill defeated Neville Chamberlain and added him to his War cabinet. President Obama defeated Hillary Clinton in the Democratic primary and then appointed her as secretary of state. President Lincoln placed William Seward at the State Department and Salmon P. Chase at the Treasury after the three waged a brutal campaign to become the first Republican Party presidential nominee. Although it may be a bitter pill to swallow, all parties need to recognize that it is in their best interests to find common ground, cooperate, and coexist.

Unfortunately, in my case, it was not my choice whether to stay at or leave Goldman. The lack of control was corrosive to my self-esteem. But I wasn't going to allow myself to seek self-destructive revenge. I wasn't going to allow myself to lash out and do long-term damage to my reputation. Instead, it was time to go into survival mode.

■ ■ ■

The feeling of getting fired sticks with you. Staring into the unknown ensures you don't take anything for granted.

Facing up to your own shortcomings is one of the hardest things to do in life. If I was honest with myself, I knew I wasn't right for that job. I knew I wasn't particularly good at financial modeling. I knew I lacked the technical skills. Most importantly, I lacked passion for what

I was doing. Even though I disciplined myself to work long hours, I was always just going through the motions. The insecurity manifested itself into a false confidence, and now that arrogant façade came crashing down. Still, I was upset. Hearing the blunt truth made it that much more painful. At the same time, with $100,000 in school debt, I didn't have much time for soul searching. There was a small sense of relief that I was escaping the torture of investment banking, but that feeling didn't last long once I began thinking about what I would do next.

After taking a day to clear my head, I ventured down to 85 Broad Street. Goldman generously allowed me to use the office to help line up another job. I started working on my resume, typing it up on a Panasonic electric typewriter. Typing 1991 as the end date to my stint helped drive home my sense of inadequacy. Walking among colleagues was even worse. I felt as if I had a scarlet letter on my chest each time I walked through the office with everyone awkwardly avoiding eye contact.

In return for their charity and the possibility of a future reference, I was responsible for passing my work over to another analyst, one who had survived the layoffs. In order to delegate my work, I had to go into the assignment director's office and drop off my files. The minute I saw him, the anger returned. I started to grind my back teeth. But, fortunately, I kept it together. I had no choice really.

Although I didn't know it at the time, the ability to suppress my anger turned out to be my saving grace. Apparently, my bosses and colleagues took notice of how well I handled the adversity and gained insights into the content of my character. As I mentioned in a previous chapter, I was rehired in a sales role in Goldman's Institutional Equity business before transitioning to Private Client Services a few years later. This second chance changed my life and set me on a more sustainable path. Keep calm and carry on—as the Brits always say—saved me.

■ ■ ■

Many years later, after I had left the firm to start my own business, one of my best friends from law school was passed over for partnership at Goldman. It was 1998, right before the firm went public. This guy had done everything right. He worked extremely hard and was incredibly smart. But his boss wanted him to walk before he ran. The night he was passed over, he called me to tell me he was going to quit. He wanted to leave the firm and crucify his boss.

"If you leave, you'll be making one of the biggest mistakes of your career," I told him. "If you bad-mouth him or the firm, the only person you'll be hurting is yourself." Giving in to the impulse to bad-mouth people only causes you to burn bridges and lose credibility. In most cases, you need your employer way more than your employer needs you.

I guess the pep talk worked because my friend never did go ballistic. He calmed down and recognized the need to communicate with his boss in a level-headed way. He'd go on to tell him he was disappointed to not be making partner but said he loved working at Goldman and looked forward to the next opportunity for a promotion in two years. It's difficult to swallow your pride and suppress your ego, but he sent a clear message: I'm a team player and you can trust me. He eventually made partner.

■ ■ ■

Even though biting my tongue at Goldman helped pave the way for my future career, I still struggled to suppress my discontent and control my emotions when office politics and bureaucracy superseded professional productivity. I'm not perfect. I have fallen victim to acting out and holding grudges. And so, in this chapter I will leave you with only one important entrepreneurial lesson—fight the urge to harbor resentment and project your bitterness in a professional setting. . . . actually, in any setting. As you will see by the anecdote below—while embarrassing to tell . . . and one that my editors toyed with removing from this book—holding grudges is futile and evoking revenge tactics only makes you look immature and green, while your adversary comes away unscathed.

Working at Lehman Brothers, I achieved a measure of success, but I made my mind up to leave in September 2004. Although I despised most aspects of the firm's culture, I wanted to be a man of my word and finish off strong. There would be no senior slide for me. I wanted to be remembered, at the very least, as a hard worker. Fond wouldn't be the right way to characterize my time at Lehman, a company that ground down both its junior and senior staff, but I wanted to make the most of a less-than-ideal situation. I read internal blast e-mails describing the retirement of a 30-year veteran in glowing terms only to hear the water-cooler scuttlebutt about what a "loser" the guy was.

At Lehman, things weren't personal, they were faux-personal. The talons were out all day, especially from those insecure about their job status—which in this case was nearly everyone. Those who aren't good at their jobs are the most insecure and the most aggressive. They seek to remove any and all threats to their job security, especially anyone who threatens to shine a spotlight on their incompetence. What is more mortifying than being shown up by an underling at an investment bank? Nothing.

At Lehman, I had a very tenuous relationship with my direct manager. He literally never returned my calls. When I asked him why, he lectured me in a condescending manner, "I learned long ago that I have to set my own agenda and control my own time. Otherwise, I would be responding day and night to subordinates, wasting my time providing comfort and unnecessary banter. My job and responsibilities are just too important for that." Apparently, whatever I needed to talk to him about just wasn't important enough. At least he dropped the passive-aggressive pretense at that point. He could have just said, "Hey, loser, stop calling me. I only return the calls of people I deem my equal or superior." That would have been more refreshing. Still, he made it clear where I stood.

In truth, although my second stint at Goldman was successful, I never belonged at a large organization. It wasn't anybody's fault, but it just was what it was. That reality became abundantly clear when I decided to play a practical joke on him.

I had a relationship with one of the longest-standing senior executives at Lehman. He was in the investment banking area but really covered the entire firm as a senior relationship manager. He was a superior to my direct boss and a jolly, highly approachable sort of guy. He had one of the best views from the 31st floor at 745 7th Avenue, the place where the head honchos hung out. I walked into his office one afternoon and asked if I could borrow his phone.

"Sure," he responded quizzically. I picked up the phone and called down to my boss. He picked up instantly, stating his first and last name in the cadence of an experienced Wall Street trader.

"Hey, since you never return my calls and I need to speak to you, I figured I would call you from up here on 31," I said. "How are you?"

Smoke must have been pouring out of his ears. I told him we needed to review the quarterly sales numbers with the regional sales managers and needed his permission, something that was hard to get since he didn't answer my calls. Needless to say, the prank didn't go over well. While we were chuckling on my end of the phone, he was livid. Suffice it to say, the episode didn't help our relationship.

As late February 2005 rolled around, I received my bonus and then I tendered my resignation. No one was surprised. My boss, meanwhile, was so happy he was ready to take George W. Bush's "Mission Accomplished" banner out of storage and pin it up in the lobby. I made a round of courtesy calls to thank everybody and say goodbye. And wouldn't you know it, this was a call my boss was certain to take.

"I am sure you heard the news."

"Why yes," he replied, "I am so sorry to see you go."

I went with it.

"Me, too, but there's something super exciting I'm working on and could use your help."

He took the bait.

"Please tell me. I will help in any way I can."

"I am setting up a sumo mud wrestling ring in the sixth floor lobby. You against me. I'm putting a satellite dish up on the roof and will charge pay-per-view to see the match. I am willing to split the proceeds with you."

He wasn't amused.

"Umm, I really don't think that's funny. You aren't saying that joke to people, are you?"

Anyway, thankfully, that toxic chapter in my career was closed. I would have preferred to hear him say, "I'm thrilled you're leaving; don't let the door hit you on the way out," but his incredulity over my joke would have to suffice.

■ ■ ■

Looking back, I probably made that joke as a defense mechanism. I was frightened at the prospect of having to leave a well-established firm and go out on my own again. But, there are NO EXCUSES. I don't want to sugar-coat this story; I wanted to tell it as it happened. I had spiraled down the rabbit hole. My emotional immaturity led me to behave maliciously, malevolently, and vindictively. And, I regret it now . . . even though it felt good at the time. In hindsight, I see clearly that I was at fault for many of our relationship mishaps. And, I regret not having the emotional maturity to just let bygones be bygones and move on.

Seeking revenge is emotionally draining and ultimately fruitless. It's one of the least productive things you can do with your time. And, if you ever have the opportunity to apologize and redeem yourself, jump on it!

■ ■ ■

My old Lehman boss, now working at a very successful hedge fund, showed up at the SALT Conference several years ago. I thought this was very big of him given our history. I sought him out at the opening cocktail party. I remembered his signature drink, ordered it from one of the bartenders, and walked it over to him.

"I bet you are surprised to see me here," he said.

He was right.

"I am, but I'm really glad you're here. Is there something I can do to make your conference experience better?"

"Well, I love OneRepublic," he replied. I reached into my pocket and handed him VIP wristbands for access to the best viewing spot for the concert. We shook hands and let our past animosity and resentment melt away. Forgiveness and reconciliation are extremely liberating. "Anger is the poison you ingest yourself, hoping it will kill the person you are angry at," the Buddha once said. When you let go of resentment, you'll feel younger and live longer. You'll also be a much better entrepreneur.

Chapter 7

An Introduction to the Important Things in Life
The Key to Living a "Rich" Life

"The years roll round and the last will comes; when I would rather have it said, He lived usefully, than, he died rich."

—Benjamin Franklin

T he assault boat hit the shore. The doors dropped and the bedlam of war began. My uncle was three rows from the door, and in the blink of an eye his life changed forever. Two feet in front of him sat a close childhood friend. A bullet flew through his head. The guy next to him, a close friend during basic training, was holding his wrist where his hand used to be. The air turned a tinge of pink as blood rained over everyone. Immediately, my uncle was pushed from behind as his fellow troops, or at least those that survived, rushed to get out of the boat.

It was June 6, 1944. American and British troops were storming the beaches of Normandy on D-Day, the operation that helped turn the tide of World War II.

My uncle fell off the boat into cold salt water. Coming off the landing platoon of the boat, he dropped his rifle as he went underwater. As he stuck his head under the water to retrieve it, he could see the streams of bullets inches from his face. The salt was burning his eyes. The noise was deafening, and yet, despite the chaos, everything seemed to move in slow motion. By the grace of God, my uncle and a few of the surviving troops from his ship made it to cover under a rock on the beach. They were pinned down by Nazi machine gunfire. They had two choices: run into the line of fire, or run into an area that was marked off in German as a minefield. The sign said ACHTUNG. Choose how you want to die, basically.

Most of the troops opted to run right into the line of Nazi fire, where many were quickly cut down. After an hour, the guy next to my uncle decided to make a break toward the "Achtung" sign, where a minefield was protected by barbed wire. The soldier cut through the wire and started running through the supposed minefield. Nothing detonated. It turned out not to be a minefield at all. The Nazis didn't have enough time to set up a firing station on that edge of the beach, so instead they set up decoys in hopes of driving the troops into enemy fire. My uncle took off running after his comrade, and they made it through the field, up a hill, and behind the Nazi gun turrets. They finally got their radios to work, calling back to their captain to let him know the minefield was safe. Their actions saved hundreds of lives.

My uncle Anthony Defeo was only 19 that day. He was a war hero and source of immense pride for my entire family, especially my Nana. He was also quite possibly the bravest person I ever knew. Just months after graduating from Port Washington High School, Anthony entered the Army. He sailed out of Nova Scotia on the RMS *Mauretania*, one of the fastest boats at the time. He was among the 5,000 soldiers bound for England. Once there, they began preparing for Normandy, which became the largest amphibious invasion in history. There was no precedent for this type of mission, and it would be incredibly difficult. Anthony's unit was charged with building docks, roads, or whatever else was needed to ensure supplies and weapons could make their way up the beach. "The Germans had everything zeroed in," my uncle would later recall. "If you ran for cover, you'd never get out of there."

Under constant fire, Anthony's unit had to keep the supplies moving from the boats to the beachheads. "There is no easy job in war," he would say modestly.

My uncle was about as decorated as a veteran can be. He received the U.S. Victory Medal, U.S. battle stars and ribbons for three different campaigns, the Good Conduct Medal, the Croix de Guerre and Jubilee of Liberty from the French government, and the Purple Heart, but not until after I saw *Saving Private Ryan* in 1998 did he tell me a single story about his service in World War II. He didn't like to talk about himself. He was too honorable to dwell on his achievements. He didn't like to brag.

What he did like to do, and did remarkably well, was raise and support his family. Until his death, Uncle Tony lived in the same house where he raised three children. I think war taught him what was really important and what really mattered. It gave him an introduction to what I call the "simplicity of life." As a young man on the beaches of Omaha, Uncle Tony saw the worst and best of mankind. He saw the randomness of who lives and dies during war, how just standing a couple of inches to your left or right could alter the course of your personal history. As a result, the little things we obsess over became less important to him. He was educated and smart, but didn't care about money or status. He could have returned home and probably had a more financially rewarding life. Instead, he worked at the local A&P supermarket as a produce manager for 40 years until he retired in 1990. He spent his entire life with one company, doing more or less the same task every day. But that didn't matter to him. Honor and family did. That's what he lived for. That's what mattered to him. When you've seen the horrors of war, you realize there is joy in living a simple life.

■ ■ ■

Uncle Tony never made decisions for money. Unfortunately, his name-sake nephew did, and it held me back for a long time.

As I mentioned previously, I grew up in a middle-class household and saw firsthand the stress that comes from an unexpected bill or expenditure. My ultimate dream was to become an entrepreneur—to be a businessman—but I also wanted to be financially independent . . . I just didn't know how. I had a naiveté about how the world worked.

The first time I saw the inside of an office was at the age of 16 when I visited my friend's dad, who worked at E. F. Hutton. The office was located at One Battery Park Place near the southernmost tip of Manhattan. We took the Long Island Rail Road into the city and number 2 train downtown. Although I was immediately intimidated by the marble floors, fancy suits, and expensive watches, I knew that I desperately wanted into that world.

In 1985, I remember reading an article in *Time* magazine about how young lawyers at Cravath, Swaine & Moore made $65,000 a year right out of law school. Adjusted for inflation, today that would be the equivalent of $150,000. That starting salary was considerably more than my father was making at the time. And so I set my sights on law school.

The path to the Promised Land seemed relatively clear to me. Get good grades in college. Check. Get into Harvard Law School. Check. Graduation. Check. And make a lot of money. . . . But here's where the dream became a little hazy.

I arrived at Harvard bright-eyed and bushy-tailed, but within the first semester I could already tell a hard truth: I hated the idea of practicing law. The endless hours of reading case study after case study put me to sleep. The need to remember the smallest piece of minutiae of some lower circuit court decision seemed tedious.

The only thing that kept me going was the promise of getting rich—and, perhaps more importantly, knowing that I was making my parents proud. Traditionally, for Italians, having a son who is a lawyer is just about the best thing in the world. I never really understood that until June of 2014 when I had the opportunity to have lunch in

Washington, D.C., with Supreme Court Justice Antonin Scalia. I mentioned to Justice Scalia how overjoyed my family was when he was named to the court in June 1986.

"What is it with Italian mothers wanting their sons to be judges?" I asked.

"Anthony, it means you're incorruptible." Justice Scalia replied. "It's proof that you aren't on the take or involved in organized crime. The only other career providing mothers with similar assurance is the priesthood."

I laughed out loud because I knew he was right.

When I came home from Harvard after my first year, I told my parents that I wanted to drop out of law school as I had no intention of practicing law. My mother was crushed. I might as well have just told her I was becoming a drug dealer. But I had slowly gained enough maturity and self-awareness to realize being a lawyer wasn't for me. Maybe it would have helped if I had come to this realization a hundred thousand dollars' worth of student loans earlier, but I'd be lucky to practice law for two years before losing interest.

But my mom wasn't having it. She talked—or, more accurately, guilted—me into getting my law degree. My lack of enthusiasm led me to fail the bar exam twice. On the third attempt I passed, but instead of setting my sights on a gavel, I decided to make a beeline for Wall Street. Besides, that's where the hot jobs were . . . the financial industry was booming.

■ ■ ■

Goldman Sachs was at the top of the investment bank food chain, so I focused my attention on getting a job at that firm. I figured I would go to Goldman, make enough money to pay off my student loans, learn a ton about the business, and eventually use my contacts to start a company.

My time at Goldman Sachs essentially served as a business school experience, except this time my bank account was moving in the opposite direction. As I mentioned previously, I wasn't a great fit for the firm, but working there gave me a stellar education in finance, ethnical behavior, and teamwork. I also met many friends, mentors, and business associates that I still hold dear to this day.

■ ■ ■

The first time I learned about the challenge of professional entrepreneurship was when I left Goldman to start Oscar Capital, an independent investment advisory firm. A lot of people thought I was nuts. I was making great money at a firm that had one of the best reputations on the Street. But I didn't care what other people thought, a trait I no doubt inherited from my mother. Labels never mattered to her. In my mother's mind, there was no difference between Oscar Capital and Goldman Sachs. All that mattered to her was that I worked hard and that I was honest. Her unwavering belief in me is the foundation for my success. My dad also set the pace with a prodigious work ethic.

After making a seven-figure salary in your thirties, it's easy to lecture people about not making decisions for money. The money and connections I made certainly helped make it possible for me to take the risk of starting my own business. Still, the decision wasn't easy. As my children grew up, I wanted to set a good example for them as someone who followed his dreams. I wanted to be able to provide a good life for them, but knew that I needed to choose uncertainty over security, entrepreneurship over bureaucracy. I was driven by what mattered to me most: the chance to build a business and realize my dream.

Of course, you can't realize a dream without experiencing a few nightmares and financial setbacks. Oscar Capital got off to a very tough start. It was the winter of 1996, and markets were experiencing their first major sell-off in years after Alan Greenspan, the Federal Reserve chairman at the time, spooked global markets with comments about the market's "irrational exuberance." Immediately thereafter, the Nikkei fell more than 3 percent and global markets soon followed. Investors began to wonder if the bubble was about to burst. The debate led to several months of volatile action, but eventually the market settled down once again.

During that time, I'd wake up each day, get dressed, read the *Wall Street Journal*, and prepare to look failure right in the face . . . and failure seemed to stare back at me, saying, "Hey kid, nice try, but I'm coming for you." I'd be lying if I said there were never times I questioned leaving Goldman, where I could have worked my way up the ladder and collected a steady, high salary. Friends would ask if I missed Goldman, and—with a forced smile—I'd tell them "no way." I was enjoying the process of building a great firm. Some of that was true. I did love what I was doing, or the idea of what I was doing. But the truth was a little more complicated. I loved it, but it terrified me . . . it scared the ever living crap out of me; all the while I wasn't even taking in a dime.

And, so, every day, I allowed myself to think about what failure really meant. I rehearsed how I would explain my decision to quit one of the great investment firms of the modern era to start my own asset management company, only to go bust in the middle of a generational bull market when all you really needed to make money was a broker and a pulse. The fear consumed me, but also motivated me to work harder, work smarter, to look failure right back in the eye and tell him, "Not today, buddy."

Eventually, I'd be rewarded. By the end of 1997, markets stabilized and our marketing efforts were paying off as we had about $200 million of new assets in our fund. Things were starting to work out. I remember closing shop one night and turning off all the lights in the office after finishing up a client call. I was getting ready to go meet my family for my mother's birthday dinner. As I locked up the door, I turned around to look at the office once more. All I could hear was the hushed sounds of computers on sleep mode, and all I could see was the glow of screen savers. It was a gorgeous sight. And, suddenly, it started to dawn on me: I was doing it, I was living out my entrepreneurial dreams. This feeling—when your company starts to turn the corner— is indescribable. It's worth more than any six-figure paycheck. No amount of money could replace what I felt at that moment.

As I went down the elevator, I thought back to my uncle, who had the courage to live his life on his own terms and follow what mattered most to him. The courage in his convictions inspired me to pursue my dream to be an entrepreneur. At times, I wondered if I was talented enough to make it work, but thinking about the things Uncle Tony overcame helped me cast those doubts aside. I was going to make my dream come true, on my terms. I walked the path of self-reliance that is the American Dream. We were on the way to building a real company.

Fear of failure continued to linger in the outer regions of my consciousness, but no longer stared me in the face. Failure was no match for the nephew of Anthony Defeo.

■■■

Don't Go into Business Purely for Money

Undoubtedly, the goal of most businesses is to make money. I get it. But, having a business that makes money and going into a business simply to make money are actually two very different things. Understanding this crucial distinction is key if you want to become a successful entrepreneur.

I started the paper route as a kid because I wanted to build something. I wanted to take pride in running my own business, just like my uncle Sal with his bike shop. He sold and serviced motorcycles. I delivered newspapers. But we were both in the customer service business. I was successful at my paper route because it was an obsession for me. I wanted to build the biggest and best paper route, and at the risk of sounding immodest, that's exactly what I did in Port Washington. And I did it through hard work. I did it through caring about and listening to my customers, creative marketing, and sheer persistence. At the end of the day, I got paid well for a 12-year-old, but it was a by-product of my thirst for entrepreneurship.

If what you're doing isn't a labor of love, you will drive yourself mad and broke. There are no shortcuts when you're starting your own business. There is no quick and easy paycheck. Mark Zuckerberg didn't become a billionaire overnight. He spent countless hours alone in a room trying to develop something that he thought could change the world. His goal was to unite people on the Internet, not get rich. The massive wealth he has created is a by-product of his vision and pride in being enterprising. The same is true of any great entrepreneur. The dream comes first, and if you're lucky, smart, and work your tail off, money will follow.

My advice is simple: If you only care about money, don't become an entrepreneur.

Tune Out the Noise & Ignore Negativity

Do you always need positive feedback and public adulation? If the answer is yes, my advice is once again quite simple—don't become an entrepreneur. If we're honest with ourselves, we've all felt the sting of embarrassment or insecurity. That's not a bad thing—admitting it shows self-awareness. The problem with worrying about your image arises when you let it dictate what you do and how you act.

The greatest innovators in history have been independent-minded, strong-willed individuals. Almost every entrepreneur—from Ray Kroc to Henry Ford to Steve Jobs to Elon Musk to Jeff Bezos—has faced public scrutiny and has been the subject of a negative storyline or media blitz. But they all had a vision that made them impervious to the opinions of the outside world, and they were willing to challenge the establishment even if it meant enduring public criticism, social ridicule, and a host of naysays. Simply put—they didn't care what other people had to say. You want to mass-produce automobiles using an assembly line? Good luck. You want to build the world's largest retail store over the Internet? That's not feasible. You want to build a super-computer that can fit into people's pockets? Impossible. If history's greatest minds had abandoned their dreams at the first sign of social rejection, we'd still be living in the Stone Age.

Before you take the risk to start your own business and create something new, ask yourself if you are willing to face public feed-back, scrutiny, and judgment. Ask yourself if you are willing to attend a neighborhood cocktail party and admit that you work for a company they have never heard of, rather than a prestigious investment bank or a super-large tech company. Ask yourself if you are willing to endure ridicule should your new business venture go south and fail.

If you have answered yes to these questions, congratulations, you are ready to be an entrepreneur. If you can take ridicule and negative opinions roll off you like raindrops, don't be afraid to take a chance and be an entrepreneur.

Turning a blind eye to the outside world is one of the hardest things to do. Although we like to think we possess the exterior of an armadillo, most people are thin-skinned. We are preconditioned to want to be liked. Most people—myself included—care what others think. But what you can't do is allow that to impact your business, your performance, your potential. I'm going to repeat this point: You can-not let what other people think of you influence your business. I can't get amped every time one of my competitors goes around telling our clients we are taking too much risk. I can't get distracted when folks in the press take potshots at me.

My business demands ultimate focus. Your business demands ulti-mate focus. And if you're worrying about what people think about you, and if you're consumed with what others are saying, you're going to become distracted and not give your business the necessary focus. What other people think of you is not important. It should not be your focus.

Of course, this mantra is easier said than done. Simply ignoring the world is difficult. I have found that you have to train yourself—as if you're training for a marathon—to tune out the outside world. Little by little, each day you can learn to ignore one thing or another. It's hard—probably one of the hardest things an entrepreneur must do. But it's necessary if you're going to be your best. Most people are bothered by personal attacks. That's why negative campaigning has become a popular strategy. It works. If they realize you have thin skin, people will attack you, especially when you are breaking new ground. You will never learn to like it, but learning to deal with it will make you that much more successful—both in your professional and personal life.

Believe You Will Succeed

Amidst all of these important lessons, there is one crucial thing to remember: You have to believe you are going to be successful.

If you believe you're going to succeed, or you believe you're going to fail, chances are you are right on both counts. Your attitude is a self-fulfilling prophecy. You must ingrain that you're going to win and succeed at your goals into your everyday thinking. Too often, insecurity and self-doubt creep into our outlook for life. We succumb to the negativity and begin to ask "why?" Why do I think I can be successful? Why would I be able to accomplish something as bold as starting a successful business?

Instead, the questions you need to ask yourself are "Why not? Why can't I be successful?" "Why can't my company get the mandate and win the business over our competitors?" I remind my team at SkyBridge of this all the time. But, the only person who can change your line of thinking is you. You need to think positively if you want a positive outcome.

Chapter 8

Partnering Up
The J-Curve They Don't Teach You About in Business School

"If I have been able to see farther than others, it was because I stood on the shoulder of giants."

—*Sir Isaac Newton*

"S o what types of things do you look for in an employee?" asked the young man across the table. Victor Oviedo was introduced to me by Eric Lane, who is now cohead of Goldman Sachs Asset Management. Victor was 28 years old at the time.

"What do I look for in an employee?" I shot back. "That's good question. . . . What do I look for in an employee?" I asked again of myself, this time more as a rhetorical question.

"Do you have a pen?" I asked. "And a piece of paper?"

While he handed over the necessary supplies, I continued, "Are you familiar with the 'J-curve'?"

"The J-curve?" Victor replied. "Yeah, I know it."

"I'm sure you know the standard definition, but we define it a little differently here at SkyBridge," I said.

The open position was for director of business development, but what I was really looking for was a jack-of-all-trades type of person. Start-ups don't have the luxury of hiring people to fit specific job functions. They typically lack the money to fill specialized roles. Instead, start-ups look for people who are problem solvers. People who can do a little bit of everything. When your company reaches a billion dollars in revenue, then you can afford to assign staff specific roles. Until that time, it's all hands on deck. You want people who will do anything and everything without complaining. You don't want to hear anyone say, "No, I didn't go to college to crunch numbers in an Excel spreadsheet or wipe down the sink in the pantry. That mentality won't work at a start-up, where everyone from the CEO to the receptionist may have to wipe down the sink.

Victor was an intriguing candidate. He had the pedigree: degrees from Wharton, Johns Hopkins, and Georgetown. He began his career in investment banking at DLJ—Donaldson, Lufkin & Jenrette. He also held positions at Merrill Lynch and Bankers Trust. Despite his success, he didn't take himself too seriously. He was highly intelligent, motivated, and creative. But what I liked most about him was that he had gone out on his own—and failed.

Several years prior to our meeting, he tried launching an Internet start-up. It failed, but clearly he was bitten by the entrepreneurial bug. I liked the fact that he had his heart broken. I liked the fact that he had suffered a devastating setback in his career and was now looking to start a new entrepreneurial endeavor, armed with the wealth of knowledge that comes with trying to start a business. You can't learn about that type of failure in business school. You have to experience it in real life. He did, and I loved that.

"All right, I know you have a gazillion degrees, so this is probably pointless for me to explain," I said as I took his pen. "But let's just review the standard J-curve."

In private equity, a J-curve is used to show how quickly investors can expect to make their money back. In the early years, most companies deliver negative returns, hence the decline in profitability as expressed by the descending curve in the first part of the "J." Over time, the heavy investment leads to decreasing losses and then increasing profits, hence the accelerating slope of the "J." After a couple of years, you're off to the races, but the first couple of months can be dicey.

"Okay, so you're familiar with this concept?" I asked Victor.

Victor just smiled and nodded, knowing something unexpected was around the corner.

"Right, well, here it's a little different," I paused for emphasis.

"Here, the curve looks a little more like a funnel," I explained, while making the bottom of the J resemble a funnel. "You see, the 'J' is here, and this guy is right below it," I said, illustrating with a stick figure. "All the shit flows to the bottom of this 'J' into this little funnel, right into this guy's mouth," I continued, now drawing an open smiley face on the stick figure. "This guy . . . well, he eats all this crap. He literally swallows all this diarrhea, and when he's not eating diarrhea, he's chomping on broken glass. You see, that's you. You're the low man on this totem pole and you're going to eat a lot of shit. But if you're willing to do that—and we're as successful as I think we can be—you're going to be wildly successful and make a boatload of money."

I had explained my version of the J-curve and asked the very same question of two other candidates. One was interested. One was appalled.

"So what do you think?" I asked.

Victor was riveted. "I can do that. When do I start?" he said without any hesitation. Two years later, he would become a partner at SkyBridge.

■ ■ ■

For me, attitude is everything. Warren Buffett said it best: "Somebody once said that in looking for people to hire, you look for three qualities: integrity, intelligence, and energy. And if you don't have the first, the other two will kill you. If you think about it, it's true. If you hire some-body without [integrity], you really want them to be dumb and lazy."

The quote could not be any more accurate. You need to be able to trust your partner 100 percent. If you don't, you won't have a successful relationship. At the end of the day, every owner has to be able to run his or her division autonomously. The CEO or founder can't always be putting out fires. You can't have 10 cooks in the kitchen for every deci-sion. Communication is important, but you need to trust individuals to make decisions.

As part of this equation, the secret to building a strong manage-ment team is finding people who are more talented than you. Hire them, share your vision, and let them do their thing. The same phi-losophy should apply at every level of an organization. As Malcolm Forbes once said, "Never hire someone who knows less than you do about what he's hired to do." In other words, every manager should hire people who are smarter than they are. There is no room for inse-curity in the workplace. When people are worried about being one-upped, it leads to a toxic, highly political environment. People are more focused on undercutting their bosses or colleagues than they were about doing their jobs. It's important to establish a team-first mentality so that every individual in your organization feels the empowerment of an entrepreneur.

■ ■ ■

Great business leaders don't credit their own genius—or some trans-formative technology—for their success. They are open and honest about the fact they can't do it by themselves. Success is not a desti-nation; it is a journey. And if you are going to build something that will live on, you have to create a culture of hiring and empowering great partners and great people. Jack Welch used to say General Electric was a bunch of small start-ups. He famously said, "If you pick the right people and give them the opportunity to spread their wings and put compensation as a carrier behind it, you almost don't have to manage them." In other words, he understood the power of avoiding the bottleneck, of putting your people in the best possible position to succeed and then getting out of the way. He let people do their jobs, and because of that he was able to be great at his.

I model my management style after Welch—or Larry Bossidy, one of his protégés, among others—with a DEA management style: Delegation, Empowerment and Accountability. Although I detail this style in Chapter 11, I will give you a quick sneak peek into this mode of thinking—specifically, how it applies with my partners.

First, I delegate. I'm not going to try to own every decision in the company. If you are going to scale your business, you have to be willing to let go and delegate responsibility, even for critical initiatives and important projects. Second, I empower my partners. I give them the resources and autonomy they need to be successful. No manager or employee should feel too intimidated to share an idea or offer constructive criticism. Third, for a hands-off approach to work, every partner, manager, and employee has to be accountable. I can't stand excuses. If I'm not going to micromanage; if I'm going to give people room to build their own small start-up, they better not take advantage of it. Unfortunately, some people have. I've had plenty of colleagues who have been dishonest or not held themselves to a high standard. People mistake kindness or patience for weakness. But, I'm always going to give my partners and team room to do what they need to be successful to take ownership of their work. When people feel in control of their own destiny, their work no longer feels like a job. It feels like a calling. That's the type of environment I seek to foster.

Partnerships can be very rewarding relationships, but in order for them to be successful, you often have to give one another the benefit of the doubt and put your ego in a jar for the betterment of the business.

■■■

The e-mail must have taken hours to craft. It was almost like an ancient text. Each time I read it, there seemed to be some new, deeper, unexpected meaning.

The "f-bomb" appeared in the same spot in each sentence. It was from my partner—Eytan Sugarman—and he was furious at me.

He concluded his red-hot missive with the simple line: "You are a **** [insert four-letter word] and a lowlife."

Wow, I thought to myself. I guess that partnership is over. I started to put the Blackberry back into my pocket, but not before admiring the finely crafted e-mail one more time. It was like a profanity haiku. How could someone get the f-bomb to line up perfectly in seven straight lines in a row? (He eventually told me he worked for four hours to get them lined up like that.)

At that intense moment the thought that this partnership might actually be over felt good.

You see, Eytan and I had been giving each other the silent treatment over our failure to raise enough money to open our new restaurant. It was our second restaurant together after the successful launch of Southern Hospitality, a barbecue joint that also counts Justin Timberlake among its partners. Southern Hospitality was a home run, which, perhaps in hindsight, gave us the false impression that opening a second eatery would be easy. But it wasn't, and we were $500,000 short of the $3.5 million needed to open our new place—the Hunt & Fish Club, whose concept was a riff on the old John Gotti Bergen County Hunt & Fish Club.

I met Eytan though our mutual friend Bobby Valentine, the former manager of the New York Mets. Eytan, Nelson Braff, Dave Barrett, and I were in charge of raising most of the money for the new restaurant. Together, the four of us formed a pretty good team, but like any partnership, we had our disagreements.

At that point, the anxiety of entrepreneurship was causing us to point fingers and project our stress onto each other. We were having trouble raising money, which, for those unfamiliar with the restaurant business, means we had hit up all our friends and business associates for equity and were all now tapped out. The inflow of money had slowed to a crawl, and in the heat of the moment, I reached for my phone and typed out a passive-aggressive e-mail detailing all the things I perceived Eytan hadn't done. I have to admit that pressing the send button gave me a cheap, fleeting sense of satisfaction. Screw him, I thought. The reality is I started the fight.

Amazingly, he didn't respond right away. Instead, he took about eight hours to craft his f-bomb masterpiece, which to this day I think belongs in a museum. Usually, when someone finds a way to insult me 36 times in a single e-mail, I sever all ties and move on. Life is too short to have a long list of enemies. But eventually I calmed down.

I was the one pointing fingers. In an impulsive moment, I blamed him for everything when, truth be told, there was plenty of blame to go around. If I was being entirely honest with myself, I fired the first shot. I should have gone to the gym to blow off steam instead of picking up my phone.

After a couple of hours and many, many deep breaths, I did the most difficult but important thing you can do in any relationship: apologize. In a business partnership, things can get heated, and then they can get personal. The best way to diffuse? Step back and depersonalize the situation.

I picked up the phone and dialed his number.

"Eytan, it's Anthony. I apologize. I was wrong. And I'd like to move forward if you are willing." He accepted my apology, and we both immediately buried the hatchet.

You can be right about everything, or you can be in a partnership. Not both. Check your ego at the door and be big enough to put out fires before they burn bridges. That said, if you find that your partnership to be draining to your business—and your sanity—you need to be honest with yourself, cut bait, and move on. Your business depends on it.

Here are three valuable pieces of advice I have about maintaining successful partnerships.

You Don't Need to Be Right All the Time

I've adapted the old axiom that you can be right or you can be married. As any couple will tell you, the key to a happy marriage isn't always about who's right and who's wrong; it's about working together. You're going to be right sometimes, and you're going to be wrong more often. How you manage your relationship with your partner or spouse will go a long way in determining how well it works. There is only one type of unconditional and asymmetrical relationship in the world, and that is between a parent and a child. All other relationships are conditional, and in order for them to be successful, they need symmetry. The best relationships have reciprocity. You don't always need to be right. When faced with a disagreement, partners should find the lowest common denominator to refocus on their purpose and mission.

Communication Is Key

People can do some amazing things, but they can't read minds. A lack of communication is often the starting point for the breakdown in a relationship. The more uncomfortable the conversation seems, the more important it is to have. It doesn't need to be a formal meeting. You just need to have an honest conversation. I must admit, I am not the best at this, but I try to work on it everyday.

Relationships Require Work

Stephen Lessing—a former managing director at Lehman Brothers and current executive at Barclays—is one of the classiest people I've met during my time on Wall Street. He is a fountain of knowledge, and if you're lucky enough to be within earshot, he'll gladly share his pearls of wisdom. My favorite line of his is "Relationships are never stagnant. Relationships are always moving, either forward or backward."

Not all relationships progress on their own, though. Relationships, even the best ones, require constant work. To have friends, you have to be a friend. You can't ignore someone for six years and then hit him up for a favor out of the blue.

You don't need to be best friends with your colleagues or your business partners. In fact, sometimes that can present problems in and of itself. But, make sure you work on that relationship. Make sure you take the time to ask them about their day, their weekend, their family, their upcoming vacation. Take the time to meet your peers for lunch and take your team to breakfast. Talk to them face-to-face. I promise you, it will pay off in the end.

■ ■ ■

"Where's Anthony Scaramucci?" asked the skinny Australian who looked like an older, more distinguished John Cusack.

I recognized his voice from our many phone conversations but had never met him in person. It was December 17, 2007. I had just flown to Australia—a week before Christmas—to meet Richard Howes face-to-face as his Australian-based firm—Challenger Life Company—was about to invest $200 million dollars in our second seeding fund. Although terms had already been agreed upon during our many con-ference calls—and we had developed a good bond—it was time to finalize the partnership . . . and flew almost 10,000 miles across the global to do so.

"Richard," I said, springing from my chair. "I'm Anthony Scaramucci. Great to finally meet you in person."

"You're Anthony Scaramucci? I was expecting a short, fat, bald Italian guy!"

"[Screw] you Richard!" is the edited version of what I said back to him with a big grin on my face.

He burst out laughing. The meeting couldn't have gotten off to a better start.

I had been introduced to Richard by a mutual friend at Deutsche Bank—John Olstein—who thought Richard would be a good candidate to invest in our new fund. Although we had a soft deal in place, Richard insisted that we meet in person to finalize the deal, which stated that his company would invest $200 million into one of our seeding funds in exchange for equity in SkyBridge. The timing was critical.

By December of 2007, the first cracks of the subprime crisis were starting to form, but the industry hadn't yet fully grasped the magnitude of the problem. In a speech just months before, Fed Chairman Ben Bernanke said the subprime problem would "weigh heavily" on the housing market but in no way "cripple the U.S. economy." The trouble in the subprime mortgage sector was "limited." Stocks were still close to record highs, but volatility had started to pick up. Two hundred–point swings on the Dow were becoming commonplace. Safe havens like gold and U.S. Treasury bonds were rallying sharply, while bank stocks were starting to act very heavy. Full-blown panic had not yet hit the market, but sphincters were getting tight. The brewing turmoil made this deal all that more important for SkyBridge.

We opened our first incubation fund with $330 million in 2006. Now we had to open another fund, and our window of time was closing fast.

After signing the term sheet, which in the hedge fund world is basically a precontract, Richard and I went for dinner to celebrate and then I flew home. Nothing was set in stone, but I felt good about the deal.

Little did I know, it was the calm before the storm.

■ ■ ■

Three months later, mayhem broke out in financial markets. Bear Stearns collapsed and it became crystal clear that the subprime lending market was in trouble. Stocks were tanking and Wall Street was entering a brave new world.

"Richard Howes is on the phone for you," my receptionist said.

I didn't even need to pick up. I already knew what he was about to say. My pulse was pounding as I reached for the phone. If Richard backed out of the deal, we were done. Finished. Goodnight. Close up shop. We would be just another piece of road kill on the hedge fund highway. Whatever he said in the next five minutes would make or break the firm.

"Listen. We have to shave back our deal," Richard said. "We can't go in with the full $200 million. But I'm still committed at $100 million."

It was a blow . . . but not a fatal wound. While half of the original agreement, $100 million was about $100 million more than I expected given market conditions.

"Richard, from the bottom of my heart, thank you." I said. "You are a man of your word."

Richard could have easily backed out of the deal—and, in the process—ended SkyBridge or at least how it was configured. All we really had was a handshake and signed term sheets. His loyalty and integrity blew my mind. Banks and hedge funds were failing all around us, but nothing was more sacred to this man than his word.

A piece of advice: If you find people who you can trust on a hand-shake, count your blessing and keep them close to your side. They are the people you want around you when the bombs go off. They are the people who honor a deal under imperfect circumstance. Richard was one of the most stand-up people I had ever met, and thank God he was the one on the other end of that deal. It's easy to have partners when things are going well. It's when things get tough that true char-acter and real friends reveal themselves.

Two days before we closed on the deal, I was at the last MLB All-Star Game at the old Yankee Stadium. The game went into extra innings and didn't end until well after 1 A.M. It was a tight, well-played game, with the American League pulling off a victory in the 15th inning. But, even I—a big baseball fan—could barely focus on the field. I kept looking around the stadium at all the people seemingly unaware of the economic crisis. Global financial markets were on the brink of collapse, yet thousands reveled in the distraction of a great celebration in "The House That Ruth Built."

Despite my faith in Richard, I wasn't ready to breathe a sigh of relief until the $100 million hit our accounts. The money arrived from Down Under a couple of days later, but it still felt like a shallow victory.

■ ■ ■

Two short months later the world of finance was really imploding, with major financial institutions falling victim to the credit crunch. Lehman Brothers filed for bankruptcy and Merrill Lynch was the recipient of a $50 billion buyout by Bank of America. The already-hemorrhaging Dow plummeted and lost an unprecedented 499 points in just one day! There was full-blown panic. While the world was watching Melissa Lee and Dylan Ratigan anchor special coverage on CNBC, I was getting on a Qantas flight back to Australia. For the second time in just one year, my business was on the brink of collapse and the same guy held our fate in his hands.

When I booked the flight a few months before, the original goal was to do more marketing with Richard and his team. However, it quickly morphed into another effort to meet face-to-face with my new partners and—not only reassure them about their new $100 million investment—but to also make sure they knew we weren't giving up no matter what happened in the markets.

"Richard," I said to him over dinner with bloodshot eyes from my 24-hour flight, "the good news is your money is in cash right now, so you haven't lost a dime. Give me a year and let's see if we can turn this around."

"We're not redeeming. I'm with you," he replied.

"Thank you, Richard. We will work tirelessly to make sure this works out for you and Challenger."

Well, the fund ultimately failed. We allocated capital too soon into the sell-off and suffered modest losses. As investors were skittish, redemptions also poured in. However, Challenger's $100 million bought us time, allowing us to survive. Richard's $100 million commitment to SkyBridge became the lunar module from Apollo 13. When all of the astronauts made it home safely, NASA called the mission a successful failure. The same can be said about this deal. While it was never used for its intended purpose, it ultimately allowed the team to remain intact . . . long enough to enable us to hop over the rabbit hole and reinvent our business.

Because Richard's commitment guaranteed him a 10 percent stake in SkyBridge, the story turned out well for him after we closed the deal for Citigroup's fund of hedge funds business and started churning out good performance. After the deal closed, I called him up.

"You probably thought you got bagged by some fast talking Long Island Italian salesman."

"No way. Listen, you guys never embarrassed me. It's a great team."

The lesson of this story is simple—there's nothing as important as meeting face-to-face in order to establish strong interpersonal relationships and partnerships. In a world of smartphones, LinkedIn, Twitter, Facebook, and Snapchat, nothing comes close to the value of a handshake, in-person dinners, and face-to-face meetings and conversations. That's what makes for great, long-lasting partnerships.

Chapter 9

Negotiating Need Not Be War

Leaving Money at the Table

"Many of life's failures are people who did not realize how close they were to success when they gave up."

—Thomas Edison

When most people think about negotiating, they are uneasy because they're anticipating something unpleasant. Negotiating involves inherent conflict. The starting point, after all, is that you want something at the expense of the person with whom you're negotiating. Negotiations to buy a house or car have relatively straight forward dynamics—here is the price at which I'm willing to buy, here is the price at which I'm willing to sell. We can try to find a suitable compromise, but if we can't, then we'll just go our separate ways. However, when you're negotiating a business deal, partnership, or salary, the dynamics become much more complex. Negotiating a partnership, for example, can result in mutually beneficial outcomes. The higher the stakes, the more strategic you need to be in your approach to negotiations.

Movies have romanticized the business of negotiation. I'll let you in on a little secret: Most negotiations don't happen at a 60-foot table on the 50th floor in a smoke-filled room. They're less dramatic. They also happen fast, so if you don't have a plan in place, you're going to end up on the short end of the stick. The most important tactic in a business negotiation is to never view the person on the other side of the table as your adversary. If you can arrive at a sensible compromise, aligning your goals with direct communication, it doesn't have to be a zero-sum game.

There are three basic approaches to business negotiations.

The Hammer & Chisel Approach

One strategy for negotiations is the hammer-and-chisel approach. It's the old-school tactic that is probably familiar to you. With this approach, you try to extract every ounce of surface value out of the negotiation. Apply relentless pressure and intimidation until you get what you want. Every dollar counts, and every percentage point counts. The tactic is common across all industries and careers. I can't stand it. People who thrive in hammer-and-chisel negotiation are hardwired for conflict and predisposed to enjoy psychological warfare. Their ability to get one over on someone validates their existence. If you're tempted to take this approach, step back and look at the bigger picture because you would most likely be better served by a softer approach. In fact, people using this tactic are sometimes rich but always miserable.

Roger Fisher Model

Roger Fisher is the late, great Harvard Law School professor who taught the Harvard Negotiation Project, an incredible class I had the pleasure of taking. He also wrote *Getting to Yes*, the best-selling book that I still use as a reference guide today. He took an analytical, objective approach to negotiating. The Fisher model explains how to remove the positional bargaining aspect of a negotiation and instead build a matrix of your wants and needs, as you try to find intersections with the person across the table. The four pillars of his approach were to separate people from the problem; focus on interests, not positions; invent options for mutual gain; and insist on objective criteria.

Before entering into any negotiation, you must always determine what Fisher called the Best Alternative to a Negotiated Agreement (BATNA). Essentially, your BATNA is your backup plan in case your negotiating partner tells you to kick rocks. If you're negotiating to buy a Toyota Camry that is listed at $10,000, but know you can get a comparable Honda Accord for $9,000, that is your BATNA. What can you fall back on if the other person walks away from the negotiation? Basically, you should be willing to accept any agreement that represents an improvement from your BATNA. In business, you should always work to improve your BATNA. Never get backed into a corner where you're desperate, or else your negotiating power will be greatly diminished.

The most powerful takeaway from Fisher's class, though, is that whenever possible, negotiations should be about creating winning outcomes for both parties. I took the course as a third-year Harvard Law student, and his teachings became a beacon that I have followed in handling negotiations and business throughout my career. How many points are you winning and how many points are you giving up? It was basically game theory approach, and for those who don't feel the need to express their manhood in the boardroom, it can be very effective.

The Li Ka-shing Approach

While Roger Fisher's negotiation principles have had a major impact on my career, at SkyBridge we subscribe to the Li Ka-shing philosophy. This approach is perhaps the trickiest, but most rewarding approach to negotiating.

It's no coincidence that the man who taught it to me—Li Ka-shing—is the richest man in Asia, with a reported net worth of around $30 billion. He rose from humble beginnings, having left school at age 15 after the death of his father to work in a plastic company. But after a lifetime of hard work, today his companies comprise 15 percent of the value of the Hong Kong Stock exchange. He's known in Asia as "Superman," largely for his vast personal network. Some call him the Warren Buffett of the East. Perhaps Warren Buffett should be called the Li Ka-shing of the West. I first met him when I started Oscar Capital and was looking to raise money.

Moses Tsang—a dear friend of mine—set up my first meeting with Li Ka-shing. The first thing Li asked me was for my opinion of the market. I was truly surprised at the line of questioning. I mean, what did some 35-year-old asset manager have to offer the great Li Ka-shing? The answer is nothing, and instead of rambling about recent news, I instead replied with a question: "What are the keys to your success? What lessons have you learned that I can apply in my own life?"

The request clearly surprised him, but not in a "who the hell is this kid" kind of way. On the contrary, he was very eager and happy to pass along his knowledge. After taking a couple of seconds to think, he told me the most important theme in his life has been his willingness to be a contrarian. When others were fearful, he was greedy. When others were weak, he was strong. When others were panicked, he was calm. Sound familiar? The Warren Buffett of the East indeed.

While Li continued to explain his core philosophy, another message started to appear between the lines: always leave money on the table for your partners. Creating partnerships and getting like-minded people to pull in the same direction is the smartest way to build a fortune. Not only will you be successful, but you will be happy. If you allow your partners to benefit handsomely from every deal, they will always come back and want to do business with you. There will never be a shortage of opportunities. The man who tries to squeeze every last nickel is never truly happy. There is a reason why so many rich people are miserable. There is a reason why some people have seemingly everything they could want in the world, but will tell you that they have nothing. For some it can never be enough. You can see it sometimes when you first meet them. They start out by telling you their balance sheet. They have a burning desire to win at all costs. Do you know why? Because that person leaves the table, often with the extra nickel, but then hates himself for not asking for two nickels. He will never be satisfied, no matter how many coins he has to rub together.

I first wrote about this philosophy in *Goodbye Gordon Gekko*, but find it important to emphasize once again to all entrepreneurs. The message is clear—be ready to create value for the person on the other side of every negotiation; it will make the business venture more successful, while creating the necessary goodwill to move forward.

In other words, when you enter negotiations, have goals beyond simple metrics. It's not just about winning. It's about creating a bond of trust and forging a symbiotic relationship. Interpersonal relationships are way more valuable than money—they are the central axiom to our existence.

You don't need to be a Chinese real estate tycoon to understand the need for a collaborative approach. It's about assessing a situation and erring on the side of generosity. To use a metaphor from my Italian heritage, it's about growing the size of the pie, not about fighting over the size of your slice. One of the keys to negotiation is that you want to get the other person to return to the table to do business with you.

During the financial crisis, Warren Buffett employed a Li-style mind-set when he invested $5 billion into both Goldman Sachs and Bank of America at a time when investors were still scared to touch financial stocks. The deals were beneficial to all parties: Buffett was able to purchase high-yielding preferred shares and stock options at rock-bottom prices, and the banks got the reputational boost needed to convince investors the firms weren't going out of business.

■ ■ ■

The Li Ka-shing approach has never proven more effective, though, than in SkyBridge's acquisition of Citigroup's Alternative Investments unit. After being bailed out in the 2008 financial crisis, Citigroup put in motion a restructuring plan that included divesting its hedge fund advisory, seeding, and fund of hedge funds units. As I mentioned previously, SkyBridge had been predominantly in the seeding business up until that point, and we had just north of $1 billion in assets under management. When I was notified that the Citi units were for sale, I knew it was a tremendous opportunity to pick up these assets at depressed prices.

In April 2010, Citigroup agreed to sell its $4.2 billion alternatives unit to SkyBridge, instantly quadrupling the size of our firm. The fact Citi sold the unit wasn't surprising given its need to streamline operations post-crisis. The shocking thing was that it agreed to sell the units to a struggling firm that was facing the very real possibility of shutting down any day. Of course, I didn't exactly tell Citigroup how close we were to closing up shop because I knew if we could get the right deal done, it could change our trajectory. The deal was a lifeline for SkyBridge, but all parties ended up benefiting in a way that would have made Li Ka-shing proud.

■ ■ ■

When I first heard rumors that Citi was looking to unload its hedge fund business in the fall of 2009, I was intrigued. Acquiring its seeding unit would give our core business a much needed boost, and the fund of hedge funds unit would allow us to dramatically expand. Before I could even entertain the thought of being able to absorb the assets, I had to get a meeting with Citigroup management, who didn't know me at all. Thankfully, we had some mutual friends.

In October 2009, I happened to be meeting a client for a drink at Del Frisco's—a New York steak house doubling as a meeting place for News Corp. executives and bankers working in Midtown. I was early and went to use the bathroom. Standing next to me were Jeff Gerson and his former business partner, Rich DiVenuto, who were top private bankers for Smith Barney. I first met Jeff years before through Blake Moore, one of my law school classmates. We had played a round of golf together at Liberty National, which, if you've ever seen me swing a golf club, might not have been the best idea. While playing a little Jewish-Italian geography name game, we realized we had several friends in common. Jeff was always a friend and stand-up guy through the years, but it had been a while since I had seen him.

Back to Del Frisco's. . . . My guests had yet to arrive, so I asked Jeff and Rich if they wanted to have a quick drink at the bar. After some small talk, I brought up Citi's hedge fund business. Given their prominent roles at Smith Barney, I figured they would know something.

"Listen, as you know, I'm running a seeding business. It's my understanding Citigroup is looking to get rid of its seeding business. I'm interested in buying it," I said.

Initially, the seeding business was the only part of Citi Alternative Investments I was interested in acquiring.

"I'll reconnect you with Eric and Ray," Jeff told me. Eric Pai created the $500 million seeding fund for the Hedge Fund Management Group for Citigroup Alternative Investments, the unit I was initially interested in buying. Ray Nolte was the CEO and CIO of that unit.

A week later, I was at 1 New York Plaza, the huge black glass skyscraper right across the street from Madison Square Garden. Jeff Gerson, Eric Pai, Rich DiVenuto, and I were sitting around a conference table overlooking the Garden and a huge poster of Tracy McGrady.

This time, we got right down to business.

"There's no chance we're going to sell you *just* the seeding business," Eric said to me.

Dammit, there goes my plan to hop over the rabbit hole and defibrillate SkyBridge. But before I even had to time to get respond, Eric said something that truly shocked me.

"The only thing the firm would be interested in would be selling the whole thing, including the on and offshore fund of hedge funds business," Eric continued.

I would like to say it was my idea to think that big and take that home run swing. The truth is it fell right into my lap. But given my grandiose ambitions as an entrepreneur, they didn't need to mention the possibility twice. All this time, I had been narrowly focused on just one part of the Citi hedge fund business, the seeder fund. Never in my wildest dreams did I think I'd have a chance to buy the *entire* business. The offer shocked me. More than that, I had no idea how we could afford the transaction. But I made sure not to blink. I had to make this work. Sometimes, good entrepreneurs have to connect the dots *after* the fact.

Now, I'm not a particularly good poker player. As much as I think I projected an air of confidence, my face probably went ghost white. I tried to clear my throat and could literally feel my Adam's apple travel through my esophagus. I looked at Eric right in the eye.

"Okay, got it. If I want this thing, it's all or nothing."

"Yes, That's the deal," Eric replied.

The next day I met with Ray Nolte in the library at the Core Club, an exclusive clubhouse for mostly Wall Street and media types in Midtown Manhattan. I sat there and listened to Ray's view of how this transaction could work out and how SkyBridge needed to position itself to be the acquirer.

"Okay," I said after snapping out of my reverie. "Let's go for it."

■ ■ ■

I was in fifth grade when quarterback Roger Staubach, one of my childhood sports heroes, popularized the term Hail Mary with his last-second, desperation heave to Drew Pearson that sent his Dallas Cowboys to victory over the Purple People Eater Minnesota Vikings defense in a 1975 NFL playoff game. The Citi acquisition was my Hail Mary. It was a canary eating an elephant. But, I did have a couple of things working in my favor—an entrepreneurial mindset and a budding brand. In addition, the size and scale of the SALT Conference—

combined with my frequent appearances on CNBC—helped convince Citigroup management that we could handle the business. We had created the perception that we were larger than we actually were, and that allowed us to punch above our weight class. Don't just take my word for it—when the transaction finally closed and the former Citigroup employees moved in, I remember one young lady was absolutely shocked at how small the firm was. She thought we had 300 employees!

"Three hundred people? Ha! In our dreams!" I said. "More like twelve, but with you guys, we're up to 35. And, we're all going to squeeze into this one floor."

(In fact, we had to get creative just to fit everyone. We absorbed a spacious conference room from a prior tenant and sectioned it off to make work stations for the new team).

As it turned out, the merger was a perfect fit. In the Citigroup team, we had an extremely talented group of people with a strong track record of performance. Our SkyBridge team was very skilled in marketing, sales, and brand development. Our core competencies complemented each other perfectly, and the chemistry was terrific right from the start.

■■■

Back to how the transaction went down. . . . There were four important factors. First, Citigroup was selling an asset Citi and Smith Barney clients were invested in, so they needed to find somebody they knew to take care of the clients. Second, Citigroup wanted to preserve the jobs of the people in the division they were selling. They didn't want to sell to another asset aggregator who would summarily fire all of those employees. They wanted to take care of their own, a concept for which I had a ton of respect. Third, because many of the clients were invested in this hedge fund business, they wanted to maintain the continuity of the performance. Citigroup didn't want somebody to switch jockeys on the clients and risk upsetting the strong performance record. A lower standard of service and performance could cause those clients, most of whom had money invested throughout various Citi businesses like commercial and mortgage banking, to rethink their overall loyalty to the firm. Finally, and perhaps most crucially, they wanted to keep their distribution and fee-sharing agreements in place on the private banking side.

In retrospect, the only reason this deal ever made it to my table was because Citi was asking for a lot. It was a very complicated, highly conditional deal that would only be palatable to the exact right buyer. Citi had entered into preliminary talks with other firms, who took a hammer-and-chisel approach, trying to extract every bit of value and dictate the terms of the deal. If I had taken a similar tack, I would have been laughed out of the room. Citi wasn't going to get low-balled, particularly from a struggling hedge fund seeder. Ultimately, Citi didn't want to make a sale but wanted to form an arm's-length partnership, and I was more than willing to oblige. By thinking back to the advice given to me by Li Ka-shing, I realized this deal could be the start of a very fruitful long-term partnership . . . one that could open doors for all parties.

In the end, despite several competing bids, we won out because of our willingness to give and take. We were taking the risk that the two cultures would be able to come together and form a cohesive and productive organization. The starting point was making the senior Citi employees who came over in the deal equity partners in the new SkyBridge, and the smooth transition proceeded from there.

Li Ka-shing would have been proud.

■ ■ ■

The lesson is clear: Don't look for the last nickel in a short-term one-sided transaction. Make sure both sides are winning when you are negotiating.

Chapter 10

Don't Hire Quarterbacks, Hire Linemen

The Simple Formula for Building a Successful Team

"There is no limit to what can be accomplished if it doesn't matter who gets the credit."

—*Ralph Waldo Emerson*

The writer in the back of the room mustered up all the courage inside him and asked Bill Parcells the question every other writer was too scared to broach.

"Coach, the Bills are averaging close to 30 points a game. They just scored 56 points against the Raiders. They obviously have a speed advantage. Do you think you have any chance of stopping the Bills' no-huddle offense?"

It was the last press conference before Super Bowl XXV. The Vegas bookmakers had set Parcells's New York Giants as four-point underdogs against the AFC-champion Buffalo Bills. Parcells—the steely-eyed Hall of Fame coach—was preparing to go up against the high-powered Bills team, who had pioneered the concept of the no-huddle offense.

This revolutionary strategy was wreaking havoc on the NFL as it often caught the defense off-guard.

There was an awkward silence in the press room. Parcells's eyes lit up. And for the first time all afternoon, he revealed his pearly whites.

Parcells didn't respond verbally at first, choosing instead to let the audacity of the question marinate in the press room for a few moments. Then his smile got bigger and his eyes appeared to almost pop out of his head. You see, Parcells lived for these moments. He loved it when people doubted him or his team. He relished the opportunity to prove the world wrong.

"If you can physically dominate," he said, "that's difficult for any opponent to deal with."

Parcells was confident because he knew something all great coaches know: the best teams are greater than the sum of their parts. Think about the great Giants teams of the late 1980s. Sure, they had Lawrence Taylor and Phil Simms, but they never had an offensive player lead the league in any category. In fact, the year they beat Buffalo to capture Super Bowl XXV, they did it without Simms (Jeff Hostetler filled in) and their leading rusher (O. J. Anderson) rushed for fewer than 800 yards. So, how'd they do it?

Teamwork.

Parcells and Bill Belichick, then the defensive coordinator of the Giants, made sure their players were in the right spot at the right time. The G-Men may have been slower than the Bills, but they turned their weaknesses into strengths. They couldn't outrun the quicker Bills, so they ran over them. They held onto the ball, controlling time of possession. They didn't commit turnovers. They played as a team. Of course, they were fortunate to see Scott Norwood's last-second 47-yard field goal sail wide right, but they made their own luck by working as a team and rowing in the same direction.

Building a business is no different.

■ ■ ■

In business, you can take a team of a modestly intelligent people and achieve more than the work of a group of extremely smart individuals pulling in different directions. The key is putting together a team with complementary skill-sets and a collective spirit. You need people who don't care who gets the credit. Your job as a leader and entrepreneur is to assemble these teams and put people in a position to succeed.

At SkyBridge, we have a ton of talented and smart employees, but we are successful because the team achieves more than the sum of its parts. Our team is a fraction of the size of many firms who manage less money because everyone at our company is willing to pitch in where needed. When the SALT Conference comes around, every member of the SkyBridge organization offers a contribution. We're lean and we're mean, and there is no task beneath us.

The best companies reward people who can be selfless at the top and are willing to subordinate their egos for the betterment of the team. Success requires an understanding that championships can only really happen with a well-rounded, self-sacrificing team. Derek Jeter understood this throughout his career. As a result of insecurity, some of his teammates never did. Gain the trust of the people around you and help create an organization that is greater than the sum of its parts.

Here are my most valuable guidelines for building a winning team.

Soap & Deodorant

The first thing I like to do is get people close. Physically close. I'm a big believer in handing out bars of soap and deodorant because you're going to work right next to your colleagues. In fact, you're going to be on top of them. I believe in Michael Bloomberg's "swamp tank" model, where people are forced to communicate openly in close quarters.

At SkyBridge I don't really have an office. There's a room on our floor containing some photos of my family, books that interest me, and memorabilia I've accumulated over the years. But, to call it my office would be a stretch—it's used more frequently as a spillover conference room. Instead, I'm constantly talking to my employees in the pit and make it a habit to randomly sit in the various SkyBridge team meetings.

As the leader, I want to see and hear everything that's going on in order to keep my finger on the pulse of the performance, culture, and morale of the firm.

Another thing I like to do in order to encourage teamwork is to assign a seemingly impossible task to new employees. Although I don't expect the person to actually complete the task, it's really a test to see how resourceful he or she can be in problem solving within the SkyBridge culture. For example, if I ask a new hire to identify the five top-perform-ing event-driven hedge fund managers on an annualized basis, I don't expect this green employee to provide a completed list within the hour. Instead, I want to see how well the employee works with her colleagues to dissect the question, analyze the research, and uncover the answer. I want to see if she asks for help or if she immediately gives up. I want to see if she gives credit to her colleagues when presenting her findings and/ or if she points the finger if the task is ultimately not completed or is done incorrectly. This may sound like a rather heinous prank, but I believe it is an effective tool in teaching employees the importance of teamwork as problem-solving tool in a high-pressure situation.

Fire First, Ask Questions Later

As I mentioned previously, I do not believe that leaders should micro-manage every aspect of their organization, but I do believe they should be held accountable for creating an office culture. The ethos of a firm starts right at the top, trickles down to every department head, works its way through every manager and director, and then makes its way to all the junior staff.

At SkyBridge, I do not hesitate to get rid of any employee if I believe he or she is poisoning the culture of my firm. If you allow uneth-ical behavior to become insidious within your organization, it becomes very hard to root out. But, I've ultimately come to regret it every time.

My friend Jim McCann—the founder and CEO of 1-800-Flowers—once told me, "I have never benefited from waiting to fire someone." That may sound harsh, but it's the truth. When you tolerate or indulge unacceptable behavior, you're sending a dangerous message to the rest of your firm. That said, I often find it hard to let members of my organization go as I worry about jeopardizing their livelihoods. Admittedly, I'm a softie. Over the years, I've tolerated some colleagues who bred dissension because they were extremely smart, productive, and creative. What manager hasn't? There were plenty of people I should have fired sooner if not for my sympathetic streak. But, I've ultimately come to regret it every time. Now, if there is evidence that someone is sowing discord at my company, I no longer hesitate to fire them. Maybe it's related to my experience of getting fired from Goldman Sachs, but it took me a long time to arrive at that point of view. Maybe it's because I always want to be the good guy and find a way to keep employees. But, I've learned that this corrosive behavior hurts the organization as well as the individual. And, over time, I've learned that ultimately you are helping the person you have to fire as you are no longer tolerating a type of behavior that will be detrimental to his or her long-term career prospects.

Simply put, managers have to send the message that backbiting will not be tolerated within the organization. If you can't get along with another employee, have a direct conversation to air your grievances or put personal vendettas aside. At the end of the day, you want every member of your organization pulling in the same direction.

Hire Entrepreneurial People

As Steve Jobs once said, "The secret of my success is that we have gone to exceptional lengths to hire the best people in the world." As the business landscape is always shifting, an organization is only as good as its employees. The status quo changes, technology disrupts established industries, and when it comes time to build and sustain your business, you need staff that have the entrepreneurial mind-set to lead your company's evolution. I don't care if you're an accountant or the head of business development, I value a self-starter mentality.

At SkyBridge, we constantly strive to reinvent ourselves and break new ground. If you want to run a successful organization, you have to find things other than money to motivate your employees. You have to find a higher purpose, a common goal that will keep people committed to the organization. For example, at SkyBridge, we pride ourselves on being the underdog. We like the fact many of our competitors are larger. We like being nimble and lean. Companies often lose their scrappy, startup mentality as they grow, but we have no desire to get to that point.

In business, you can either refuse to change and get "Blockbustered," or you can "pull a Netflix" and be entrepreneurial, evolve, and hop over the inevitable rabbit holes that you encounter. You can stubbornly resist change or reinvent the way you do business. Netflix used to mail DVDs and now its streaming service accounts for nearly a third of the nation's broadband usage. In the coming decades, more media companies will come along to disrupt the status quo, and Netflix's survival will depend on management's ability to instill an entrepreneurial culture, composed of staff who are willing to adapt and evolve.

The transition wasn't all smooth sailing for Netflix, though. How was Netflix CEO Reed Hastings able to get his team to buy into his vision when the stock was tanking and being targeted by short sellers? He was able to articulate to his employees that their work was bigger than a paycheck. He was able to impress upon them that there was light at the end of the tunnel, that if they could execute properly they would revolutionize the way people consumed media and watched television. He offered individuals a chance to be part of something bigger than themselves. That's how you build a great business.

Learn from the Best and Bravest

If you want to develop an effective and well-run organization, you need to study elite people and organizations. You need to look at the Amazons and Apples of the world. You need to study entrepreneurial icons like Mark Cuban, Arianna Huffington, Jack Welch, and Elon Musk. And what better group of people to study than the U.S. military, unquestionably one of the greatest organizations in the history of mankind?

I come from a family of servicemen but am part of a non-service generation. Every one of my elders either enlisted or got drafted into the U.S. military—four uncles and one very proud father. Their generation didn't view service as a sacrifice, they viewed it as duty, something every American does. It was part of life, much the same way college is part of life for many people today.

For my generation, the mentality was different. The closest I ever came to serving was signing my draft card back in 1982 when I turned 18. I never thought of doing the Reserve Officers' Training Corps (ROTC). The draft had ended. Vietnam had ended, and even if it hadn't, I don't think I would have volunteered if I'm being truly honest with myself. Military became a four-letter word in the 1970s. As a result, if you were born between 1960 and 1980, you probably never seriously considered enlisting. You certainly didn't give it serious thought if you had a college degree. Fast forward to today, and many Americans' separation from the military has grown even wider.

Less than 0.5 percent of the U.S. population today serves in any of the armed forces. During World War II, nearly 12 percent of the population was in the military. Even those casting the votes to send young American men and women are further removed from service. In 1975, 70 percent of those serving in Congress had some form of military service, owing largely to WWII. Now, that number is just 20 percent. During WWII, nearly half of the nation's economic output was derived from wartime services and manufacturing. People conserved and were encouraged to use ration stamps. Women joined the workforce to help make warplanes and weapons. Rosie the Riveter was revered. General Motors cut back on making automobiles for consumers so it could supply the military with jeeps and trucks. Everyone put aside their differences and came together as Americans to fight a common enemy.

Could you imagine these types of sacrifices today?

War is something most people talk about, but many don't truly understand the gravity of war. Of course, we pay armed service men and women obligatory lip service. We salute them at ballgames and talk about the "real heroes," but as a society we can do more for our best and bravest Americans.

In fact, a lack of gratitude has begun to permeate our entire society. This is a mistake, not just from a values standpoint, but also a business perspective.

I learned this firsthand through my experience with the Business Executives for National Security (BENS). BENS is an outstanding organization that allows business leaders to offer their expertise to the military in efforts to rebuild war-torn areas. I joined at the behest of my late friend and mentor—Joe Robert—and am now a board member. BENS has not only given me a front-row seat to how the military operates, but it also has given me an education in courage, entrepreneurship, and leadership.

In January 2011, I made a trip to Iraq on a BENS-sponsored trip. I'll admit—I was terrified. We were there on a press junket that included a stop at Baghdad University to talk about entrepreneurship. We were led by retired four-star general Montgomery Meigs. I learned about the casualty rate. I learned about the sectarian violence. I learned about something called ISIS—well before it became an international story three years later. The trip was eye-opening, to say the least.

After the tour, we retired to our quarters in the Green Zone. I was restless, so I decided to fit in a workout. After a few miles, I stepped off the treadmill to get a drink of water and for the first time noticed the pictures on the wall. They were pictures of young service men and women, all looking roughly the same age as my oldest son. I was looking at a memorial. It broke my heart.

Service members embody moral exceptionalism. They are trained to run toward the gunfire and into burning buildings. Through my involvement with several veterans' organizations, I've met many of these brave men and women, and their courage never ceases to amaze me. My trip to Kabul, Afghanistan in October 2015 only fortified this view. We are blessed to have these men and women serve our country.

I'm an unapologetic patriot, and I truly believe these American service men and women are the greatest people in the world. The love they have for their country, the pride they take in their work, and the selfless way they think about service is astounding. And they possess every single trait a business would want in an employee.

Complete subordination of self for the benefit of the team and mission? Check. Physically and mentally prepared beyond anything you could imagine? Check. Calm and assertive in the face of adversity? Check. Willing to make great sacrifices for the sake of a greater good? Check.

I can't imagine a better model to learn from in order to build a great business and foster a culture of collaboration and teamwork.

Chapter 11

Person to Person
From Management to Corporate Citizenship

"A leader is best when people barely know he exists, when his work is done, his aim fulfilled, they will say: we did it ourselves."
— *Lao Tzu, Chinese Philosopher*

I f you are interested in learning about the United States during the Golden Years, I encourage you to pick up a copy of *The Man in the Grey Flannel Suit.* You'll get a sense for an America of white shirts, thin ties, blue and gray suits, wingtips, and corporate conformity. Because postwar corporations were chock-full of returning soldiers, a command-and-control philosophy was effective and accepted. At that time the United States had very little competition for world economic domination, having seen most of the developed world decimated by the horrors of World War II. Essentially, the United States was a global manufacturing monopoly at a time when demand for goods was exploding. The powerful combination of increasing supply and demand created real wage growth and the rise of a financially secure middle class. People took pride in living a modest life. If you had a small home, car, TV, and home-cooked meals, you were living the good life.

With all that was going on in the country, a command-and-control management style worked well. The rise of technology, however, has made management much more complex. In today's world, newer management principles are now the norm.

■ ■ ■

As I mentioned in Chapter 8, I model my management style after Welch—or Larry Bossidy, one of his protégés—with a DEA management style: Delegation, Empowerment, and Accountability. But in order for this style to be successful, you must also seek to create a culture of morality and properly manage the inevitable politics that plague every organization.

Delegation

Technology has changed the world at an ever accelerating pace. In the workplace, Internet-based applications have created more collaborative environments and reduced bureaucracy, but many business leaders still insist on maintaining a command and control management style. I call that leadership style the monopolist manager.

Monopolist managers are typically insecure, petty, paranoid, and surrounded by "yes men"; however, they would be better off building the team into a cohesive unit and fostering loyalty, creativity, and commitment. They would be better for mastering the art of delegation.

Having a boss is an inevitable part of professional life, but studies show that employees feel stifled by bureaucracy and micromanagement. Accountability is important, but you first have to trust your process to find good people and then delegate essential roles, responsibilities, and tasks to them. Obsessive managers believe nobody can do a job better than they can. Great managers accept that they have to delegate to get things done. The regimented soldier-like mentality does not apply.

Empowerment

Ronald Reagan had a brass plaque on his desk in the oval office that said, "It is amazing what you can accomplish if you do not care who gets the credit." When I first read this quote in *Fortune* magazine in the mid-1980s, I scoffed at the notion. I was jaded by experiences from my early career when I saw the most cutthroat and brown-nosing people get ahead. I didn't have the stomach to become that type of person, and their success, frankly, bothered me. As I got older and became a business owner, I finally started to understand the true meaning of this saying.

True leadership requires personal subordination. As Lee Iacocca—who pioneered the development of the Ford Mustang and then took Chrysler from the brink of bankruptcy to become a global powerhouse—once said, "I hire people brighter than me and I get out of their way." In other words, you have to put yourself in the position of facilitator. People need to know you care about them, and that goodwill will translate into good work. True empowerment requires trust and personal subordination.

The SALT Conference, again, is a great example of how we apply this philosophy within SkyBridge. In addition to being our head of business development, my partner, Victor Oviedo, is effectively the CEO of SALT. He picks the date and the venue, he sets the budget and agenda, he dictates the speakers and content, and, most importantly, he picks the band. Kelly O'Connor is his partner in that business—and all of our brand-building initiatives—and they run every aspect of the conference with an extremely small team. Yes, the rest of the partnership group makes suggestions but we give them the leeway to make final decisions on anything within the realm of SALT. As a result of the freedom we have granted them, they take great pride and ownership in putting on a great conference every year.

Similarly, my co-managing partner—Ray Nolte—and I provide Troy Gayeski—the senior portfolio manager on the SkyBridge flagship investment products—with the same autonomy. While he receives considerable guidance from Ray, Troy is granted the intellectual latitude to take ownership of our portfolios. Ray and I share a philosophy of empowerment, which became apparent from the first time we met to discuss the initial acquisition of his unit from Citigroup.

Ironically, even though I am the founder of the company, I see my job as more of a supporting role. I think about how I can help the process, but mostly I stay out of the way. Empowerment requires that release of control.

Accountability

As a leader, I would prefer to accept the blame for any major company missteps. If my team is putting in an honest effort, I am happy to give them credit for things that go right, but also willing to shield them from blame for things that go awry. That said, empowerment doesn't work without accountability. If someone takes ownership of a project or division, he or she should receive credit when things go right; and he or she should be willing to take the blame when things go wrong . . . even if the person isn't personally responsible for certain outcomes. You can't have your cake and eat it, too.

Ultimately, great leaders let the buck stop with them. If you want to earn your stripes and become a leader, I'd suggest you doing the following things:

1. In a crisis, don't cower. Accept responsibility for any wrongdoings and take the heat off others.
2. Don't finger-point . . . it's a sign of insecurity. Instead, focus on diagnosing and fixing the problem, not assigning blame.
3. Focus on operating from a place of integrity. Character is revealed and legacies defined by how you respond in times of adversity. If you make everything about money and status, you will lose the locker room when bad times hit.

Creating an Ethical Culture

Excuse me for a minute while I get up on my soapbox. Wall Street has a terrible reputation. Some of it is deserved and some of it is stoked by politicians and the media. As an industry, though, it is our responsibility to shed the negative stereotype by creating a higher standard of ethics. We have all heard the Italian cliché "the fish stinks from the head down." If you want an honest group of people around you, act with honesty. None of us are perfect. Introduce me to the person who claims to have never told a lie, and it will be easy for me to point out the biggest liar in the room.

■ ■ ■

If you join SkyBridge, you have to listen to the following story:

None of my ancestors worked behind a desk. My grandparents were masons, mechanics, grocers, cafeteria workers, and laundry operators. While my dad eventually got a desk job later in life, he started out as a construction laborer. Everyone in my family who came before me took great risks to put me in a position to rise above my station in life. Everyone bought into the American Dream. They didn't envy those with more than them, those who worked half as hard and made ten times more. They were grateful for the opportunities given to them. You didn't see the type of class warfare we see stoked by politicians today. For my family, the most important thing was to make sure their kids and grandkids had the same or greater opportunities to make their own way. Education was extremely important. In my mind, the most powerful thing my family passed on to me was a last name with a reputation for integrity. I learned early on there is nothing more valuable than your name and reputation. There is never any reason, especially money, that should cause you to jeopardize your name. I have three sons and a daughter who will use my last name. They deserve it intact. No amount of money or status is worth losing it. Anyone inside the organization that is even close to the ethical line will be fired.

I tell this story to all my employees to help guide their professional—and, even, personal—conduct. And I also give them the same message about the SkyBridge name. The firm has never received a bad mark from regulators, but it takes only one bad act to tear down a reputation that took a decade to build. There is no gray area here. Cross the line and you are finished.

■■■

Politics & Perceptions

"I want my organization to have zero politics," I told my dad. "A place where there are open lines of communication and people don't get bogged down in petty sniping." I was still naive enough at age 32 on the eve of starting my own business to actually say something like that.

My dad looked at me and laughed.

"If there are more than two people in the room, you have politics." I have never heard a truer statement in my life. Whether you're in a large corporation or a small family business, you will encounter politics at both the top and the bottom. One-on-one relationships don't have politics. Two people communicate directly. But when you bring an additional person into the mix, the nature of that relationship automatically changes. In a group of three people there are in effect five relationships—those between the individuals and a collective one. The more people you add to the mix, the more permutations and friction.

The driving force behind most politics within an organization is insecurity. When people are not doing their jobs—or doing their job poorly—they worry about colleagues finding out. They strike preemptively to make other people look bad and to deflect attention from themselves. The result is a workforce of employees doing whatever it takes to protect their own ass, rather than working together for the common good.

■ ■ ■

All organizations, both big and small, have politics. It doesn't matter if you work for a large organization like Disney or a local diner. You are never going to be able to root out back-biting and insecurity at all levels of your institution, but as a leader you must foster a culture of open communication, transparency, and teamwork by implementing the DEA management style.

Remember, conflict is not the same thing as politics. Conflict is healthy. It means people are communicating and holding each other accountable. Problems arise when people surreptitiously undermine each other. Talking behind someone's back breeds distrust, which kills any semblance of collaboration.

The key to fixing the culture within your organization boils down to three Cs: command, control, and collaborate. Politics are inevitable but can be minimized if you create an environment where people feel empowered, productive, and secure.

At SkyBridge, we have a "kiss down, slap up" philosophy. I surround myself with people who challenge and question me. Debate is healthy in the workplace. Passionate disagreements are the lifeblood of an organization. As a leader, allowing people to question you sends an important message to the rest of the organization that nobody's ideas are infallible and constructive feedback is essential for development, scalability, and success. President Lincoln was famous for bringing adversaries into his cabinet. It helped him become a better leader. He surrounded himself with a diverse set of opinions and voices. Too often in corporate America, CEOs and leaders surround themselves with "yes men." That said, once a decision is made, as a teammate, you need to support the process.

■ ■ ■

Here are three simple rules that you can follow to stay above the fray and avoid the pitfalls of politics.

Rule 1: Don't Take Anything Personally

While I was at Stanford University showing my son the campus, I noticed that companies were setting up tables to recruit students for jobs and internships. There were rows of tables, each with a corporate logo and a very clean-cut representative in a finely tailored suit. They were all giving out business cards and trying to explain to these future Masters of the Universe why they should join their company. All the big banks and law firms were there, plus dozens of tech companies. Amid the group, I spotted a competitor of SkyBridge accepting resumes.

I told my son to go over to the table and act as if he were interested in learning about the firm. Right when the recruiter was about to give him collateral, he would say that he was going to take a job at SkyBridge. I admit it was kind of juvenile. I suggested that Victor join him, but he had to wear sunglasses to cover the wrinkles around his eyes.

My son's execution was flawless. He acted eager to learn about the potential job and asked engaging questions. About 15 minutes later the recruiter leaned into him and asked, "Hey, can I send you some information about our firm? I think you'd be a great candidate."

My son, acting as flattered as possible, politely declined and said, "I'm thinking of taking a job at SkyBridge Capital. They've made me a pretty good offer. Do you know their founder, Anthony Scaramucci? He's fantastic."

"Fantastic?" the recruiter replied. "He's the guy who's always going on TV pretending to know what he's talking about. The guy's a douchebag. You don't want to work for him."

My son immediately burst out laughing, shook the recuiter's hand, and came back to me.

"Dad, you're not going to believe what he said." He laughed uncontrollably. "He called you a douchebag."

"No way," I laughed. "That's hysterical."

Ten years earlier, being called a bad name would have bothered me. I would have tapped into my inner Italian. I might have walked over to the guy and shouted at him for insulting me and my firm. Instead, I calmly introduced myself, flashing a genuine smile the whole time.

"How are you? I'm Anthony Scaramucci." I said. "I'm the guy you just called a douchebag."

"Oh, you're Anthony Scaramucci," the guy says to me, in a high-pitched, nervous voice. He looked like he was about to piss his pants.

"That's me. Hey, please take my card. I would welcome the opportunity to change your opinion about me at some point."

The reason I was able to laugh about the incident was because after countless years of getting angry at small stuff, I finally learned to embrace one of the most basic and fundamental rules of being an entrepreneur—don't take anything personally.

Earlier in my career, I took everything personally—how people looked at me, the assignments I was given, even the way other people dressed often seemed like a vague insult to me. "That guy is wearing a $3,000 Brioni suit and I'm not—he must think he's better than me." I was in desperate need of a shrink. Looking back, that mindset hurt my career. For all the success I've been blessed with, I could have had a lot more without all the anxiety. Taking everything so personally caused me to make irrational decisions. It took me over a decade to develop a sense of self-awareness. Don't make the same mistake and waste that valuable time.

That's why I am sharing these stories with you—to wake you up! It is actually painful to be this revealing but if sharing my shame will help you to minimize your self-doubt, then it will have been worth it. Never be intimidated. We are all the same.

If you're going to "make a dent in the universe," you're going to have to survive a few barbs. Steve Jobs never felt the need to be adored, and now neither do I.

More than once I've been ripped apart by bloggers and reporters. One particular instance really bothered me. (If you want to read it, it's still at the top of the Google search results if you search my name.) The day the article came out I was headed to the Lupus Foundation annual luncheon with the New York Jets. I was sitting at owner Woody Johnson's table with Donald J. Trump. Sensing my downtrodden demeanor, Mr. Trump turned to me and asked me what was going on as he had never seen me this way.

When I told him about the article, he said, "Look, it comes with the territory. You are gaining a high profile, which means it's time for people to start shooting at you. Buck up! Big deal you were raked over the coals a little bit. So what? It has been happening to me for over 30 years. I laugh at the hit pieces now. The sooner you build up your resistance, the better." He was right. Since that moment, I have tried to ignore the verbal buckshot and the social media screeds. I admit I'm still not completely desensitized, but the occasional negativity doesn't bother me nearly as much.

At first, this can be a hard rule to follow because much of what goes on in the workplace feels personal. After all, it becomes hard to separate the professional from the personal as you spend so much time in the office and build so many relationships. All the while, you are competing for promotions, raises, and bonuses against the very people with whom you are supposed to collaborate. It's an environment inherently ripe for conflict. As a result, people are going to say and do "mean" things. You have to accept that there are going to be people out there attacking you, but you can't let it affect your own behavior or ethics. Worry about the things you can control and accept the things you cannot. Take your own work ethic and character personally, but don't live or die by what other people think about you.

Rule 2: Avoid the Cabal of Negativity

Misery loves company, and within an organization, few things bring people together more than complaining about their bosses and their colleagues. Although it seems easy to fall into the trap of bad-mouthing your peers and gossiping about other employees, don't let yourself succumb to this sort of negativity.

I like to call people that fall into the cabal of negativity the proletariat gripers. Every office has them. They are anti-authority by nature, distrusting of their superiors, allergic to structure and rules, and, as a result, constantly bitching and moaning. In most cases, they are talented and productive, but never likely to get far in an organization because of their overly critical mind-set. They bring other people down and damage morale. As a young person in an organization, you might be tempted to join that crowd, to ease your own angst by sharing your frustration with others. That's not a good idea. Do not let gossip and negativity consume you.

Reputations take years to make and seconds to break, and if you get pegged as a complainer, that stigma will be hard to escape.

Rule 3: Scout Out the Influencers

Do you remember the great Peter Sellers in *Being There*, the fabulous film adaptation of Jerzy Kosinski's terrific book? If you don't, go watch the movie and read the book. Kosinski tells the story of "Chance"—a simple gardener who has spent his entire life tending to the plants of a rich man's estate. When that man dies, Chance is pushed into the real world, where people mistake his simple-minded utterances for profoundly brilliant simplicity. In truth, Chance is a moron whose only knowledge of the outside world comes from television. By his own admission, he can't read or write and simply likes to watch TV. But, that doesn't stop him from eventually becoming a top adviser to the president.

In one scene, the president asks Chance when he thinks the economy will start growing again. Chance, who can only talk about the garden he's been taking care of his whole life, responds by talking about his plants.

"In the garden, growth has its seasons," Chance says. "First comes spring and summer, but then we have fall and winter. And then we get spring and summer again."

After a long pause, the president appeared impressed.

"Hmm. Well, Mr. Gardner, I must admit that is one of the most refreshing and optimistic statements I've heard in a very, very long time," he told Chance. And after a second, he concluded, "I admire your good, solid sense. That's precisely what we lack on Capitol Hill."

The point of the scene is that politicians' views are often impacted by their limited number of influential advisers. If you want to have a large impact on an organization, you have to be part of the inner circle. The best way to get there and climb the ranks is to be your own consistent, authentic self.

To get on the right track, it's important to figure out who the influencers are in your company. Who are the two or three people who have the ear of your manager? Identify them. Get to know them. Make sure they respect you because their impression of you will color your boss's perception. They are going to be either your ticket to a promotion or your ticket out of town. As I said before, all business is local. Bosses don't rely on advice from dozens of people; they trust managers to deliver news. They trust a select few lieutenants to be their eyes and ears. In trying to figure out just who the influencers are, don't simply go by the organizational chart—observe and listen for the opinions that matter within the firm.

If influencers in the company are not your biggest fans, figure out a way to change their perception. Look for situations where you can connect with them personally. Make clear to them your willingness to work hard and sacrifice for the firm. That's not politics. That's common sense.

Chapter 12

Image Is Everything
Owning Your Message

"There is only one success—to be able to spend your life in your own way."

—Christopher Morley

"This is the best [effing] party, man," exclaimed the junior associate to a group of Goldman Sachs senior managers after emerging from the bathroom, hair disheveled and reeking of booze. For emphasis, he felt compelled to reiterate the point. "I mean like, [effing] ever, man."

It was near the end of the year. Up until that point the young man had a good reputation within the firm. He was seemingly a straight-edged kid—Ivy League alum, smart, hardworking. But that entire façade came crashing down when he started drinking. In an instant, the diligent professional turned into frat boy. The more drinks he put down, the faster he ruined his hard-earned reputation.

"Dude, you know what we need at work?" he mumbled to one of his bosses, a mild-mannered senior executive who wore a slightly bemused smile as he enjoyed the spectacle. "More tail like that," he said, gesturing to his boss's secretary walking by. That comment was the straw that broke the camel's back. The executive walked away and asked that the young man be sent home.

He wasn't fired right away, but for all intents and purposes he was done at the firm. He stopped getting invited to meetings. His bosses stopped assigning him work. He was isolated. Right after he learned he wasn't getting a bonus, that his job prospects at the firm were nonexistent, he quietly left, relegated to a punchline and cautionary tale about drinking too much at the company holiday party.

Harsh? You bet. But that's life. If a kid doesn't have enough self-control to behave at a company party, how can he be trusted to work on multibillion-dollar deals or to keep quiet about a confidential transaction? You can't, and in business, liability trumps all.

■ ■ ■

Much like your personal life, the arc of your career will be determined by a number of crucial moments and decisions. As often as possible, you have to be the best version of yourself so that when those moments come, they turn out positive. While you may be a good person "deep down," how people perceive you plays an important role in determining your lot in business and in life.

The most important step in building relationships is getting comfortable with your authentic self. After you've embraced your vulnerabilities and learned to cope with your shortcomings, you can change how you are perceived.

There are forgivable and unforgivable offenses. You can't get wasted at the company holiday party and vomit in the bathroom or bring three strippers to a holiday party. If you're having a tough time in your personal life, don't self-medicate with drugs and alcohol, especially in front of work colleagues. Trust me, nothing positive will come of it.

I'm not moralizing. I've made plenty of mistakes in my life. But keep your dirty personal laundry out of the company hamper. If you make an honest effort, do the right things, and demonstrate an ability to learn from mistakes, you will be on the right track.

■■■

Contrition, the mea culpa, is one of humanity's most sacred acts. The same goes for forgiveness. In order to rehabilitate your reputation, improve your image, and get a second chance, you have to first be willing to admit wrongdoing and be accountable. In a professional setting, you have to be able to walk into your manager's office, apologize, and accept responsibility—sometimes even if it isn't completely your "fault." When you are accountable and willing to accept blame, you're telling your managers you are a standup person worthy of trust, which is the most important quality in a relationship.

You can't go halfway on a genuine mea culpa, you have to be all in. Mea culpas demand full ownership.

Companies also have the power to alter their reputations, but it requires the right corporate communications strategy. To be successful in the corporate world, you need everybody pulling in the same direction, and you need the world to hear that story.

Prior to SkyBridge's acquisition of Citigroup's alternative investments unit, our core business—the hedge fund seeding fund—was on the brink of closing . . . and our clients knew it. After the acquisition, we realized the need to reshape our firm's narrative, further define our brand, and market ourselves more boldly. Immediately, we devised a strategic plan that would inform the public of SkyBridge's new business offering—fund of hedge funds products—and our pioneering role in the alternative investment arena. It was time for us to establish SkyBridge as industry experts in the world of hedge funds and define who we were before other people did it for us.

So I went on TV and radio. I conducted interviews with industry and mainstream media outlets, including the *Wall Street Journal, New*

York Times, Hedge Fund Alert, and *Institutional Investor.* We evolved the SALT Conference.

Although I didn't expect the increased exposure to be all positive, SkyBridge suddenly became part of the story. Of course, not all of the press or feedback was positive, but the fact was that SkyBridge was starting to matter. We became a household name.

We also actively engaged our customers. More accurately, we smothered them in superb customer service. We hit the road, employing a Sam Walton–like approach to marketing. We focused on small cities like Tuscaloosa, Alabama, and Davenport, Iowa, because we thought those cities were underserved markets. I didn't want our team to focus only on competing against the other big asset managers for money. I wanted to bring high-quality alternative investment solutions to people who previously had no access or exposure to them. In our model, small customers were valued just as highly as large ones. Once we had a modest base of capital, we could demonstrate our expertise to the world, and the rest would follow.

Slowly but surely, the strategy worked. Our reputation changed, our performance improved, and people talked about us differently. We started a positive feedback loop that helped SkyBridge nearly triple in size.

Although I'd like to think we're geniuses, we really just followed a time-tested approach to staging a turnaround. It has been done millions of times before with both big and small companies alike.

Remember when people thought Johnson & Johnson was dead and buried? In 1982, seven people died in Chicago after taking cyanide-laced capsules of Extra-Strength Tylenol. The pain-reliever accounted for 17 percent of Johnson & Johnson's net income the previous year and was the company's best-selling product. Marketing experts predicted the brand would never recover, that people would never take Tylenol again. Tylenol's market share soon fell from an industry-leading 37 percent down to 7 percent. But instead of throwing in the towel, Johnson & Johnson set about fixing the problem and changing the narrative. Tylenol was back on the shelves within 60 days, this time with a tamper-proof top. At the same time, the company launched a massive media campaign to build awareness of its new safety measures. A year later, Tylenol had recaptured 30 percent of the pain-reliever market.

How did the company do it?

First, they took ownership of the mistake despite the fact the issue was related to tampering. By taking responsibility, the company maintained at least a semblance of trust with customers. They took the time and paid the money ($100 million) to pull 31 million bottles from shelves. They didn't panic and point fingers—they made bold decisions first and asked questions later.

Second, the company's chairman, James Burke, didn't hide. He was decisive and went in front of the camera. He talked directly to his customers, explaining in a detail what had gone wrong and how the company would fix the problem. At the time, the aggressive approach was revolutionary. Before 1982, product recalls were extremely rare. Forty years later, J&J is stronger than ever and the Tylenol incident is a case study in crisis management.

■ ■ ■

Entrepreneurs and founders must make it their business to implement strategic and effective marketing strategies that will ultimately shape the way clients perceive the brand. Below are three rules you should follow when trying to manage your—and your company's—image.

Rule 1: Mount a Public Relations Strategy

An effective public relations strategy is one part controlled—through advertisements—and one part uncontrolled—through the media.

As a controlled strategy, ads are designed to make consumers associate a certain feeling with a product so that they are more likely to take notice. Advertisements can help, but they have to embody your company's vision for the world. When Boeing or General Electric advertises on *Meet the Press*, they don't try and sell you a turbine or a plane. They talk about how aviation is changing the world and how alternative energy production is saving the planet. The spirit of the ads is aspirational.

But, to me, the key to an effective public relations strategy is media. In order to take this strategy from potentially uncontrolled to controlled, you must develop a relationship with the press. A classic mistake that some entrepreneurs and business owners make when someone is writing a story about them or their company is to make like an ostrich and offer a "No comment." Never do that. You have to respond; invariably it will make the piece more objective. That said, you can't control everything that is written and said about you, but by making yourself a resource and opening a dialogue with journalists, they're more likely to give you the benefit of the doubt or be willing to hear your side of the story. When you pay for an ad or write an op-ed, people always look at the content with skepticism. Of course you are going to paint a positive picture of yourself. When an independent third party writes a story about you, or seeks you out for a quote on a big story, it is a much more powerful affirmation of your credibility and expertise.

When we first started the SALT Conference, many media outlets didn't take us seriously. As mentioned in Chapter 1, it wasn't until year two that the media took interest in large part because of our great content and lineup of relevant, newsworthy speakers. And after a couple of years, the media had no choice but to cover SALT. Reciprocally, we went out of our way to provide the media with access to our speakers and noteworthy events. *New York Times* reporter Peter Lattman wrote a front-page story in the newspaper's business section about the conference, describing the event as a potent mix of business and celebrity that was "above all else, a good time."

At the same time, you can't expect the good without the bad. We've had our share of tough press, too. We do our best to put on a good show with great content, and let the chips fall where they may. As long as coverage falls within a reasonable range of honesty, I don't bat an eye. In fact, sometimes I enjoy the critical stories because they help reinforce the idea that we can never rest on our laurels. Besides, sometimes the press provides extremely valuable feedback and good ideas. It's okay to be vulnerable. Vulnerability makes you more approachable, and to grow your business you need to connect with your clients.

Has our media strategy been solely responsible for our firm's growth? Of course not. But has it been an important part of our formula? You bet.

Rule 2: Build a Culture of Communication

Outspokenness will generate a good amount of press, but to truly scale your business you need to build a culture of communication and hire a team that is committed to this initiative. It's beneficial to have a balance of personalities within an organization. At SkyBridge, there are obviously many talented employees who handle our back office, and even brilliant members of our investment team who aren't public figures. But you should have a team of people within your organization who are able to get out and tell your story.

In the past decade, the growth of the Internet and digital media has dramatically changed the asset management industry. The competition for assets and standard of performance has never been greater, and the trust from clients has never been more fickle. To gain and maintain market share, you have to maintain constant communication with current and prospective clients. You have to shape the narrative around your company because if you don't, your competitors will do it for you. That means taking the time and spending the money to travel across the country meeting in-person with investors big and small. That means leveraging things like social media to communicate.

The world has changed. You have to be your own advocate. You have to bring your message to the market using whatever method makes the most sense.

Rule 3: Have Killer Customer Relations

Forget the 24-hour news cycle. Today, we live in the 24-hour surveillance cycle. Between cameras and social media, every person in the world has the same production and distribution capabilities as a major media network. As a result, your business is just one tweet, one Facebook live video, or one Snapchat away from oblivion. An airline stewardess makes a racist remark that's caught on camera, and the next thing you know people are boycotting the company. Say the wrong thing at an off-the-record political fundraiser and you better believe it will find its way onto the Internet. Social media also raises the stakes of customer service. Piss off the wrong customer, and you could face a tsunami of public backlash.

At SkyBridge, we pride ourselves on customer relations. In many cases, we devote double the resources of our competitors to customer relations. Still, we could always be doing a lot better. The world has become too small and too flat to tolerate shoddy service. Even with all our efforts, we still get things wrong. Donald Porter once said, "Customers don't expect you to be perfect. They do expect you to fix things when they go wrong." That applies to most people and is true in most walks of life.

Chapter 13

Networking, Sprezzatura, & Being Your Authentic Self

The Keys to Building Relationships

"There is no royal road; you've got to work a good deal harder than most people want to work."

—*Charles Wilson*

I t felt like a wake. All first-year analysts had gathered on the top floor of Goldman Sachs's gleaming office tower for the opportunity to meet and schmooze with company directors and executives. Beer, wine, and hors d'oeuvres were served, but to call it a happy hour would be to insult the word *happy*.

Everybody was nervous, scared to say the wrong thing to the wrong person. Anonymity, they figured, was better than someone finding out your name for the wrong reason. I was part of that insecure and anxious group. "Just blend in," I thought. "Please don't let them notice me being too awkward and realize I don't belong here."

By the end of the event—after a lot of forced smiles, cursory hand-shakes, curt hellos, and obligatory small talk—the number of contacts I made was a big fat zero. The hospitality staff made a better impression than I did.

As I sat at home that night, I was disappointed in my perfor-mance. I was disappointed that I wasted such a great and rare oppor-tunity. I was in a room with some of the most influential people on Wall Street for the express purpose of building relationships, and I couldn't bring myself to have a meaningful conversation with a single person. Sure, I introduced myself to a few people, but I didn't con-nect with anyone who would remember me in an hour—let alone a week later. Instead, I gravitated toward people who I knew in my associate class—mistake #1; talked strictly about business—mistake #2; and failed to hand out a single business card—mistake #3.

That night, I promised myself I'd never make these mistakes again. One of the things that I had going for me was my affabil-ity. My congenial disposition basically got me through lots of rough patches over the years. What I lacked was self-confidence . . . the belief that I belonged in that room. I felt like a fraud who would be exposed at any moment if I said the wrong thing. I was convinced everyone was watching and judging me all the time. I was fixated on the thought that everyone else had a nicer suit than I had, came from a wealthier family than I did, and was better than me. The first two facts might have been true, but it took me several years to real-ize those things didn't make one person better than another. Sure, I finally changed out of polyester into wool. But—perhaps, more importantly—I realized that my humble upbringing was actually an advantage, providing me with the hunger and motivation to chart my own path. And, now, I tell my kids not to take anything for granted and to work hard. Otherwise, some middle-class grinder will be com-ing to eat your lunch.

In hindsight, the networking opportunity I wasted that night was a blessing because it served as a wake-up call. I wasn't done making mis-takes in my career, but no longer would I fall short for lack of trying.

■ ■ ■

There is no skill more vital to an entrepreneur than networking. I owe everything I have built in my career to my ability to forge genuine, reciprocal relationships. Networking opens doors—both personally and professionally. If you're not networking, making new relationships and building upon existing ones, you're doing a general disservice to your career. Networking needs to be as much part of your routine as brushing your teeth. Even the nicest house or car needs regular maintenance or else they will deteriorate. And, after a while, networking becomes second nature. For me, building relationships and helping people is the most enjoyable part of my career. Especially in a world where social media has all of us focused on Facebook rather than on face-time, your ability to connect with people on a personal level will differentiate you from your peers.

Once you get to a certain age and stage in your career, what matters most is who you know and what you've done lately. Strong personal relationships are also more durable than business-only relationships. When you can humanize yourself and open up to someone else about your vulnerabilities, the person is much more willing to trust you. That said, networking should not be approached as a way to get something out of another person. It should be viewed as an opportunity to make an exchange, which doesn't always have to be symmetrical. By getting to know someone, you figure out what they truly want and how to make yourself a valuable resource.

Of course, networking isn't easy for everyone. The less practice you have and the longer you put it off, the more intimidating it becomes. For many people, it doesn't come naturally. Although it's okay to be more introverted, a failure to step out of your comfort zone and form relationships will come back to haunt you personally and professionally.

Fortunately, there are several simple steps you can take to make the networking process easier.

Train Yourself to Go First

When I was in that room at Goldman, I kept waiting for people to come up to me. As a defense mechanism, I avoided eye contact for fear it would spark another awkward conversation. I didn't want to face rejection, so I rejected other people first. Looking back, I realize how childish that view was. The truth is that in any situation where you feel uncomfortable, most of the other people in the room are probably feeling the same way. Most people play it safe in an effort to avoid making a bad impression, and in the process make no impression at all, which is a mistake.

Break the cycle. Force yourself to do something uncomfortable. Find someone in the room, go over to the person, and introduce yourself. Keep it straightforward.

"I'm Anthony Scaramucci. I work in equity sales. It's really nice to meet you."

After a firm introduction, everything gets easier. The person will likely be grateful you made the first move, and you can begin to build the foundation of a relationship built on trust and reciprocity.

Don't Talk Business

If you're starting your own business or getting hired by Google, chances are you excelled academically at a good school and/or distinguished yourself in another way. When you get in a room full of your peers, it's easy and natural to gravitate toward topics on which you have shared experience. The problem is conversations about work rarely allow you to build the kind of personal relationship that will grow and last.

Even in settings outside the workplace, it's better to drive the conversation away from business. By simply being at the same ballgame or at the same bar table, you've tacitly acknowledged the desire to build a business relationship. But for that relationship to move forward, you will have to develop a level of trust that can be cultivated only by more personal dialogue and interaction. In order to build that camaraderie, I encourage all entrepreneurs to follow the following three steps.

First, think about setting. Meeting someone in a conference room while you're both wearing suits isn't as valuable as meeting them at a bar, café, or Mets game where the conversation can be more relaxed. Second, the conversation should be meaningful, but lighthearted. The last thing someone wants to hear at a Knicks game is how you're growing your regional sales figures. It is a place to lament the fact the Knicks haven't had a real point guard since the Carter administration. Whatever you choose to discuss, try to find common ground. Third, the best way to forge a business relationship is to ask for advice. People love offering expertise, and people feel good about helping other people. When you ask someone for advice, you're tacitly acknowledging them as an expert in a field or subject. That in itself makes them feel good. Someone who is made to feel good is more likely to help you.

Put Yourself in a Positive State of Mind Before You Enter a Room

After I wasted that golden networking opportunity at Goldman Sachs, I realized the problem had been my mind-set entering the room. I psyched myself out for no reason, viewing the occasion as a source of anxiety rather than excitement. Before you enter a situation that you perceive as stressful, there are mental exercises you can do to reverse your psychology. Repeat positive affirmations to yourself: "I belong here"; "I have worked hard to get here, and this is the beginning of a long, successful career"; "I am in control of my own destiny"; "I am extremely fortunate and grateful for the opportunities in front of me."

Studies have also shown that even just forcing yourself to smile can translate into a more positive mind-set. So can physical movement. Get up and walk around during the day. Work out in the morning if you have a big day ahead. You may think you can fake positive energy, but people have a sixth sense. Just like you can only build lasting relationships if you act like your authentic self, you can only make a positive impression if you give off an authentically positive energy. If you become known as a positive person who gets along well with people, colleagues will gravitate toward you and view you as an influencer.

Follow Up within Two Days

As a rule of thumb, I usually try to contact someone within two days after we meet. If you wait a week or more, you let the initial connection fade. The follow-up should be simple and to the point, a quick e-mail about how much you enjoyed meeting the individual and an invitation to continue to the conversation. Keep it short and sweet, and never try to solicit business right away. The follow-up e-mail is simply a way to consolidate the relationship, which may or may not result directly in a future business transaction. If the person doesn't respond initially, follow up a few weeks later, but always keep the tone conversational and positive, not demanding.

Networking Should Be Fun

Believe it or not, networking can be fun, and I'm not talking about the free food and drinks. While networking can help advance your career, you don't need to treat it like work. In fact, done properly, after a while networking won't even feel like a chore.

Tap your alumni association. Reconnect with former classmates; it may lead to conversations and relationships you never expected. The Harvard Club and the Core Club have been invaluable tools for me in meeting new people and reconnecting with old friends. Relax and don't be bashful.

Get Referrals

Not every person with whom you connect will be able to directly add value to your career or life, and that is not how you should view relationships. Building a relationship is personally rewarding, but also increases your derivative connections. Once you have developed rapport and trust with someone, it is much easier to get referrals.

Referrals will almost always exceed the number of personal relationships a person can maintain. Knowing a lot of people reinforces your credibility and trustworthiness with people you are meeting for the first time. However, it takes time to build a relationship to the point where you can ask for referrals. As with a follow-up e-mail to a networking event, don't immediately solicit business. If you start asking someone you've just met for referrals, he or she will realize your intentions are shallow. This is the worst part of sales: the implied transparency. It doesn't have to be that way. Don't make it a focus; just relax. Only once you have reached a comfort level with someone should you ask the person for referrals. After a certain point, he or she will be more than happy to oblige.

If you expect people to provide you referrals, you have to be willing to open up your network, too. You should have no problem going first.

Never Be Intimidated

This important rule extends far beyond networking. Believe it or not, I'm actually a shy person by nature. If you've gotten this far into the book, you're probably groaning at that suggestion. The truth is, despite my public persona, I'm most comfortable when reading or writing. I'm most in my element when sitting in a library or study. Being shy isn't a bad thing. I think it comes from wanting to be liked but also from introversion. However, there is a difference between being shy and closing yourself off to the world. I have pushed myself to be more extroverted. In general, I am interested in what people have to say. Over time I've become more comfortable in public situations.

A big reason I feel that professionals sometimes feel intimidated in recent years is because of the lack of personal interaction in today's world due to e-mail, smartphones, and social media. Networking opportunities—such as conferences—provide the opportunity for people to take a break from the overstimulation of technology and tap into the social coding that has been in our genes since we lived in caves. Many people have forgotten what it's like to sit down, look someone in the eye and get to know them. In a twist of irony, despite our increasing number of connections on social networks, we've forgotten how to be social and network.

Overcome Your Insecurities

I've been around so many talented business executives whose careers were held back over insecurity. I know because I used to be one of them. When I started at Goldman Sachs, I felt inferior to my colleagues, despite having excelled at Tufts and Harvard Law School.

The night before my first day at Goldman, I couldn't fall asleep because of the crushing anxiety. Walking into the iconic office at 85 Broad Street, I was immediately intimidated by the surroundings. . . . and, the clothes. Everyone seemed to be wearing finely tailored Armani suits, perfectly matched their Ferragamo belts and shoes, expensive cufflinks, and exquisite Hermes ties. Meanwhile, I was wearing a wool suit and Sy Syms was my fashion consultant. The shoulders were a little too broad, the cut too boxy, the pants too loose, the lapels too thick. I wore a simple red and blue striped tie. I looked like I just got out of school and grabbed whatever was in my closet, which, in fairness, was exactly what I did.

I felt like everyone was staring at me in amusement, when in reality nobody likely noticed or cared. I was fixated on the thought that everyone there was better than me, even though we all went to the same schools and many came from modest backgrounds. And the Goldman partners scared me the most. They had an aura of power, like they were part of the Illuminati. It took me a long time to muster the courage to even put together a sentence in front of these high-level employees.

The biggest actual difference between "them" and me at that point was that I didn't know how to confidently handle myself. I lacked what the Italian classicists call *Sprezzatura*. Originating from the Italian classic *The Book of the Courtier,* the best way to describe Sprezzatura is the ability of a duck to kick furiously beneath the surface of the water while looking smooth and graceful above it. It's an idealistic nonchalance. That's what these guys had . . . and what I lacked. You would have thought all my fancy degrees would have given me self-confidence, but they didn't.

As I mentioned previously, these are painful passages to write, but, again, I am trying to reach you, to give you a lesson I wished I had learned long ago: Be confident and positive and things will work out.

I know it's a cliché, but it's true. We are all just human beings. The realization that helped me finally get comfortable being in a room with powerful people was simple: everybody's shit stinks. I used to subscribe to the notion that rich people were somehow superior. I believed somehow being wealthy helps eliminate all problems, anxiety, and insecurity. Now that I have my own company and financial security, I realize that everyone has problems, everyone has insecurities, everyone has fears. If somebody had given me this lecture when I was buried under a mountain of student debt, I would have told them to save their breath. But it's true. Given time and perspective, I realize now that we're all the same.

When I was rehired into Goldman Sachs' sales division, my job was to build a relationship with some of the richest people in the world and convince them to invest with us. Sounds simple, right? Well, there is no manual for establishing trust with a billionaire.

When I walked into my second first day at Goldman, the feeling of dread and insecurity washed over me once again. I had some practice coping with the cutthroat environment, but perhaps getting fired had reset my brain and erased any progress I made on the self-esteem front.

One sales visit in particular made a big impression on me and helped me start to realize that rich people weren't super-human. I was sent to visit a wealthy client in Connecticut. He had started and sold a tech company for a ridiculous sum of money and was apparently looking for the best way to invest his bounty. The guy's house (actually compound would be a better word) was this exquisite structure right on the water. I had truly never seen anything like it. It wasn't an ostentatious display of wealth, but rather an incredibly elegant and stately manor. The landscaping alone must have cost hundreds of thousands of dollars a year.

So there I come, chugging up to this tasteful palace in my powder blue 1987 Honda Civic. The bumper was scratched up, but not as bad as the driver's side door. There was a big dent in the rear bumper courtesy of the New York City public garage. The interior touches included a missing radio, manual roll-up windows, and a nonfunctioning air-conditioning unit. The anxiety had already started to take hold of me before I even stepped out of the car.

By the time I got to the front door, I was overcome with this horrifying realization: "Oh my God. I work at Goldman Sachs. I'm supposed to be this big shot, and I drive quite possibly the world's ugliest car. I should get something new, a Mercedes or a BMW, but then again I don't have any money." I made a good salary at Goldman, but I was still paying off school loans from Tufts and Harvard, where I got an expensive education on why I didn't want to be a lawyer.

When I knocked at the door, the butler—yes, he even had a butler—cut right to the chase. "Are you here to sell insurance?" he asked.

"No, I'm here from Goldman Sachs. I have an appointment," I said, biting my lip to hide the anxiety bubbling up inside me.

"Just a moment," he replied, leaving me alone at the doorstep. I turned around and looked at my Honda Civic behind a backdrop of well-manicured gardens.

Two minutes later my client arrived at the door. As we shook hands and exchanged pleasantries, I prayed he would quickly turn around and walk back inside before catching a glimpse of the Mooch-mobile. But then it happened. His eyes zeroed in on the heap of junk over my shoulder, and a ping of embarrassment shot down my spine.

"Is that your car?" he asked.

"Indeed it is, sir," I replied with a sheepish smile on my face.

"Let me ask you something. Do you have any money?"

"Money? I have absolutely no money, sir."

He immediately burst out laughing and invited me in, proceeding to tell the story of his modest upbringing in Australia. His story was not all that different from mine; it took him 25 years to build his business up from nothing. That's right—an overnight success takes about 25 solid years of hard work. He seemed more amused by his newfound wealth than anything else.

Once we started talking, the anxiety melted away. I no longer felt the nagging inferiority complex. We weren't so different. In fact, I think my modest circumstances and vulnerability helped me make a connection that eventually resulted in a hefty sale.

■■■

Today, I spend time with all kinds of powerful and accomplished people, and it's not always true that everyone maintains humility in the face of power. Some people grow, others swell. One of the first things we do out of the womb is develop facial recognition skills. We need to identify our primary caregiver in order to survive. As we get older, those facial recognition skills help us figure out emotions and empathize with people.

In most of our day-to-day interactions, we experience symmetrical relationships. You talk to a person, that person responds, and each party is an equal participant in the conversation. When you are around a celebrity, the connection is asymmetrical. Simply being in the vicinity of a famous person is enough to make a "regular" person giddy.

I remember my first encounter with a major celebrity. It was 1995 and there were few bigger superstars than Arnold Schwarzenegger. He had just finished *Terminator 2* and a series of successful comedies. In addition to movies, Arnold also had a number of real estate and other business investments, including a restaurant in Santa Monica called Schatzi on Main. The lunch was set up by Bobby Shriver, Arnold's brother-in-law and my client at Goldman. I had inherited the account from Roy Zuckerberg, who had a long-standing relationship with the Kennedy family. Bobby was every bit the gracious, smart, generous gentleman as his old man, Sargent Shriver.

Bobby set up a meeting with his sister Maria Shriver and her husband at Schatzi's. I got there early, and shortly after Arnold and Maria pulled up in a big black Hummer.

His hand felt like granite, which I guess shouldn't have been a surprise considering he had destroyed communist armies, jumped through walls, and manhandled aliens. He was a physical specimen, unlike any person I'd ever seen.

"Hello," he said in that unmistakable deep Austrian accent. "I'm Arnold. Nice to meet you."

Despite his intimidating stature, he was remarkably friendly and outgoing. This was before his stint as governor of California, but I could see why he would become a successful politician. However, in spite of his considerable charm, I was still extremely nervous. Would Arnold like me? Did he find me interesting? Was I just another hanger-on who wanted a celebrity friend? I felt extremely self-conscious, similar to those first few days at Goldman.

But there was something else. It wasn't Arnold or Maria, both of whom could not have been nicer or more gracious. It was the fact that I was sitting across from the Terminator, a guy who I had watched on the big screen for so many years. In fact, as he was talking my mind drifted to the time I saw the movie in the theater. And, his familiar voice—imitated by countless late night comedians—would set me out of my dreamlike trance. It was like an echo, the real voice bouncing up against what I thought it would sound like.

Eventually, I settled down. After lunch, he gave me a tour of his office, which was filled with tons of priceless movie memorabilia.

We had more in common than I thought. We both came from modest backgrounds and placed an emphasis on never forgetting our roots. In his office, he actually built a replica of his childhood bedroom in Austria. He said it put him in touch with his upbringing, and was often a place he would go to reflect on his life and success.

"You can't just think about things, Anthony," he told me at one point. "You have to just do it. I wanted to be a movie star, so I did it."

The more time I spent in his company that afternoon, the more my anxiety and intimidation wore off. He was just a regular guy who tapped into an incredible drive and will to succeed. He had discipline. He had passion. He was kind. I felt we shared certain qualities but had simply applied them in different fields. Getting to know Arnold helped me further acclimate to being comfortable with people who I perceived to be more powerful than me.

It was years later that it dawned on me that we all have more in common than what separates us. And now when I get approached in restaurants by viewers of my show, I always make a point to talk to them, give them my card, and mail them copies of my books. I am a firm believer in leaving a trail of good karma in my wake. It is a simple rule—just be nice.

If you can embrace the fact that people are equal, you'll enjoy life and be more successful. You won't feel intimidated. You'll meet more people. You'll feel more confident, not only in your skills, but also in your ability to make decisions in both your personal and professional life. It's a process. The best thing you can do is take it day by day.

Chapter 14

Sell without Selling Your Soul

"I'm a great believer in luck, and I find the harder I work the more of it I have."

—*Thomas Jefferson*

"Hello, ma'am. I was wondering if you were interested in possibly buying some of these seeds from the American Seed Company. My name is Anthony Scaramucci. I live down the street. You see, these seeds are special . . ."

The door slammed shut before I could even start my pitch. I certainly wasn't born a good salesman. At 11 years old, I was nervous, uncomfortable, and insecure, but I had ambition and dreamed of big things. And on Long Island in the 1970s, a sales job seemed the best way to climb my way to the top.

One day I was reading a comic book and came across an ad for the American Seed Company. If you sold enough seeds, you could send in your ledger and the company would send you a choice of highly coveted gifts. I had my heart set on a cutting-edge Casio watch that not only had fancy features like a timer but could tell time in Paris,

London, and Tokyo. It might as well have been my generation's iPhone. The plan was simple: sell enough seeds and send in my credits for the watch. The only problem was that I didn't know how to sell.

The whole sales process felt wholly unnatural to me. It was like being forced to play the lead role in the school play when you had a fear of public speaking. It felt especially phony because I didn't believe in the product I was selling. I just wanted the watch. Fortunately, my neighbors understood the situation and were generally kind and ultimately helped me improve my sales skills. Once I got more comfortable and let my personality come through, I started selling more and more seeds.

Despite securing my coveted watch—which I still have—the experience didn't exactly make me realize sales was my calling. As I got older, I realized there was a certain negative connotation to being a salesperson. When I thought of salesmen, I thought of the self-loathing Willie Loman in *Death of a Salesman* or the four unethical agents in *Glengarry Glen Ross*. They were caricatures of overaggressive, immoral hustlers looking to con people.

The reason for this negative portrayal is that the career itself is somewhat unnatural. The livelihood of salespeople depends on their ability to sell products, but not every customer may want or need what they're selling. The asymmetry creates a false sense of authenticity because you are attempting to separate people from their money, which creates an awkwardness and, at times, an artificiality to the relationship. However, if selling is done ethically and honestly, it is not a tug-of-war. It is about providing someone with something they may need or want.

I love sales. I enjoy selling because when I'm selling I'm actually not selling. Instead, I am building a relationship. I'm building trust. As Mark Cuban said, "Selling is not asking; selling is helping others." And that's the secret. Effective and rewarding sales is about building long-term symbiotic relationships, even if there is never a direct financial exchange. It's about avoiding the friction that results from that false sense of urgency and the incongruous nature of the salesman-customer relationship.

You don't need a larger-than-life personality to be an effective salesperson. You don't need to stay out all night and drink your clients under the table to close multimillion-dollar deals. You simply need to learn how to build trust with people, while being your authentic self.

Sales is about relationships. If you master the sales process, you will feel happier, more secure, and more self-actualized. You will be confident that whatever happens in your life, you will find a way to succeed.

■■■

The trouble for most people is that they often do not view themselves as salespeople. That is a mistake. We all are. At some point in your career—regardless of your position—you will need to sell. In my nearly 30 years on Wall Street, I have found sales to be one of the most rewarding things I've done. It's allowed me to build meaningful relationships that extend far beyond business. It's given me the opportunity to meet some of the most interesting people in the world.

One of the reasons I've done so well in sales is that I've never tried to sell anyone anything. I've simply taken pride in the process of learning about people so I could better suggest a product that met their objectives and needs. Before ever talking business, I try to find common ground and build a relationship based on trust. If they are not a good fit for the products I'm selling, I don't push. I know that I have the law of numbers on my side. SkyBridge's internal sales training is based exactly on that premise—be a good person and become a resource to your counterparty.

■■■

Many professionals are fearful of selling because they are afraid to hear the word *no*. Human nature is to fear rejection. Both through nature and nurture, we are taught to stop when we hear the word *no*. In fact, I think *no* is the most powerful word in our vernacular. However, the best salespeople learn how to take the word *no* and make it work for them.

I'll use an example to illustrate my point. You take a prospective client out for a round of golf. You make all the right jokes, develop a strong rapport, and keep the match close but let him win. After the round, you head up to the clubhouse to drink, eat, and shoot the breeze. When the moment seems right, you bring up the investment opportunity.

"That sounds like an interesting product," he says. "I'm interested in learning more."

Suddenly, he begins to ask a few inquisitive questions. Your answers are on point. He's nodding his head affirmatively.

Now you're getting excited. You have his attention in a relaxed setting and he seems engaged. You scribble on the back of the cocktail napkin to make your pitch, explaining the reasons why this is the right investment and the right time for him. He seems to be picking up what you're putting down. You even start to count the chickens before they hatch, calculating in your head how much you could make on the transaction.

Finally, after more contemplation, the potential client says, "I really appreciate you showing me this. But right now it's not right for me."

The reverie is broken, and you do a quick double take. Did he just say no? What just happened?

"But thank you for sharing the idea and having me out here today," he adds.

A forced smile comes across your face as you try to mask the disappointment. But now you've reached the moment of truth for a salesman. The next 15 minutes will make or break you. At this point, you have a few options.

Retreat and Hide

By tucking your tail between your legs and walking away, you make it clear to the prospective client that you were never interested in forming a relationship. You simply wanted a quick payday, and now that he isn't giving it to you, you have no use for him. This is the easiest thing to do at the point of initial rejection, but also the most damaging—both for your professional and personal development. Not only will you have no chance of making that sale in the future, you will have closed yourself off from that person's network. You will have started a negative feedback loop that impairs your courage to go first.

Try Again

Although the client may have said that he wasn't interested, you think you can change his mind right then and there. For salespeople who have overcome their own insecurity and fear of rejection, this is the most common response. However, when someone politely declines an offer, the last thing he wants is for you to apply pressure. Just like retreating and hiding, being overly persistent will lead to distrust and prevent you from building a relationship. The hard sell never works because it does not facilitate a meaningful transaction. You never want someone to feel like he was sold something, you want him to feel as if he gained something and is the one who took advantage of a tremendous opportunity. If the person feels positive about the transaction, he will be a customer for life, and will refer you to future customers.

Turn "No" into "On"

The word *no* should not be scary. In sales, *no* isn't a bad thing at all. When the person to whom you're selling says the word *no*, that is when the relationship and transaction begins. I often tell newer salespeople at SkyBridge that if you want to raise $500 million, you need at least $3 billion in no's. I love the word *no*.

When a baseball player gets a hit 30 percent of the time, he's considered an All-Star. The reality is that even successful people fail more than half the time. In sales, when you strike out, you don't have to walk back to the dugout. You get as many at-bats as you can muster. If you're batting average is low, make up for it in volume. Schedule 20 meetings per day instead of ten. Even after that initial rejection, you get to continue the dialogue. When someone turns me down, I look for other ways I can make myself a resource. I learn what the person really wants and needs and help him solve problems in ways that may not directly benefit me. I'll send the person a SkyBridge hat or fleece, not because he desperately wants SkyBridge-branded paraphernalia, but because it says to that person, "I care about you and want to maintain a relationship."

Sales is all about building a relationship with a person to the point that when it comes time to sign on the dotted line, it doesn't feel like a transaction. It feels like a reciprocal exchange of value. You should be wary of the person who never tells you no, not the ones who do.

■ ■ ■

Let's go back to our golf-loving client . . . after an enjoyable round of golf, he has just successfully resisted your advances and decided not to invest in your new business venture or fund. Being a seasoned sales-person, though, you shake off the disappointment, look him in the eye, and say, "Maybe now isn't the right time for you, but I really appreciate you listening. I'd love to stay in contact and get another round of golf in sometime."

Your next move is perhaps the most important step of all: ask for a referral.

"This fund may not be right for you, but can you think of anyone who might have interest? And if you do, would you be willing to make an introduction?"

With the goodwill you built up from a successful day of network-ing and relationship building, that prospective client is happy to pro-vide you a referral. Now the relationship is not simply about money. It's about a mutual exchange of information.

At that point, you and the prospective client have entered the Triangle of Intimacy, which is the foundation of all relationships.

Trust

Karma   **Reciprocity**

The Triangle of Intimacy cannot be built in one conversation, one day, or even one month. It takes time and effort to build up good karma and establish reciprocity, which both contribute to the strong sense of trust that underlies all meaningful relationships.

Trust

You cannot be an effective salesperson without establishing trust, and the best way to develop trust is by displaying vulnerability. By showing self-awareness and revealing your own anxieties, you open up lines of honest communication. When you show vulnerability, the person across from you is likely to respond in kind.

The most vulnerable moment in my life came when my daughter, Amelia, was sick. She had a tumor that was literally breaking her right arm and stunting its growth. A surgeon would have to remove the tumor and then surgically add more than an inch to her arm. It was every parent's nightmare. I racked my brain trying to figure out who in the medical community could help me. At the time, I had a good relationship with Keith Banks, who is now the CEO of U.S. Trust. I used to cover Keith when I was at Goldman and he worked at JPMorgan. Keith and I were friendly but didn't socialize. When I told him about my daughter, he didn't hesitate to help and suggested I make contact with Dr. David Roye at Yale.

Our pediatrician—Dr. Fred Barash—knew Dr. Roye and said he was one of the best doctors in the country at performing this particular procedure. I bring up this story partly to brag again about my daughter—who is one of the bravest people I know—but also to make a point. Ben Franklin said it best, "If you want to make a friend, ask that person for a favor." I exposed my vulnerability to Keith. He saw me at my weakest, and I saw him at his most generous. It allowed our relationship to extend beyond simple business transactions. It changed my view of him, but more importantly, it changed my daughter's life. I can't ever repay him for what he did for my family. The point to remember is when you're in sales, you're really in relationship management. You want to develop trust, and the best way to accelerate that process is by displaying vulnerability.

■■■

Steve Jobs was perhaps this century's greatest inventor and business-man, but he was still deeply scarred by the fact that his parents gave him up for adoption. He talked about never getting over being abandoned by his parents, never shaking that feeling that he wasn't good enough. Why didn't they want him? Those feelings nagged at Jobs even though he was adopted into a loving and supportive family. Although he transformed multiple industries, he harbored deep vulnerabilities, but he didn't allow them to hold him back. They fueled him and made him more human, allowing him to establish trust with those he worked with. Without suffering heartache early in his life, he probably wouldn't have become a technology and business icon. There was a ton of vulnerability there, and it made him uncomfortable. But he used it to his advantage. Many people didn't like him, but he was an incredible motivator because most people could relate to him and trust him.

Reciprocity

The second point on the Triangle of Intimacy is reciprocity. There's a great book by Robert Cialdini, *Psychology of Influence,* which explains the idea that if you want to have influence over someone, you must establish reciprocity in the relationship. Meaningful relationships can't be one-sided, and saying thank you isn't enough. That doesn't mean the exchange has to be financially equal; it just means both parties must put forth an effort.

The beginning of reciprocal relationship, though, requires one person to go first. If I do you a favor, you are much more likely to help me in the future. If you do me a favor, I am much more likely to want to return it. Once favors have been exchanged, a sense of trust starts to build. Personally, I like going first and am not a big believer that things have to be linear. Just going first and doing the right thing is a good place to start.

Again, it's important to understand that reciprocity isn't the same as quid pro quo. Just because I do something for you doesn't mean you have to do something for me. Never do a favor for the sake of getting something in return. Take a long-term view of relationships.

Karma

The third point of the triangle is karma. Many aspects of life are out of your control, but one thing you can control is how you treat people. Everywhere you go in life, leave a trail of good karma. Litter the world with people for whom you have done favors without expecting anything in return. In sales, there are selfish reasons for spreading good karma. You never know from where your next customer or referral will come. You could be in a restaurant sitting a table over from your next client, and the way you treat your server will reveal important details about your character. In fact, the waiter could be your next potential client. As Wayne Dyer once said, "How people treat you is their karma; how you react is yours."

■ ■ ■

When I first started at SkyBridge, I used to take a lot of meetings and do a lot of networking at the Harvard Club. As a result of my upbringing, I always made a point to treat everyone with the utmost respect and dignity regardless of their profession. My grandmother came to this country with nothing and worked several jobs to provide for her family. She turned beds and waited on people, so when I see someone working hard in a service job, I think about my grandmother. I think about how I would have wanted someone to treat her. Nothing upsets me more than people who treat those "below" them with a lack of respect. How you treat people reveals a lot about your character. Treat the people serving you with kindness.

In any case, there was one particular young man who worked at the Harvard Club who assisted me pretty much every day. He and I developed a great rapport. We'd always talk about the daily headlines in the news and often joke about the misfortunes of the Mets and Jets.

One day the young man approached me and timidly asked, "Mr. Anthony, sorry to bother you but do you have a moment? I need to ask you some advice."

"Of course," I responded. "What can I help you with?"

He proceeded to tell me that his family had just won a $35 million medical settlement as a result of his son being badly injured in a chemical spill. And, now he needed help managing the money.

"I know you work in the finance industry. Would you invest it for me?" he asked.

I'm rarely at a loss for words, but the question really threw me. First off, I was flattered that of all the people in the world he could have turned to for help, he came to me. I was honored that he thought highly enough of me to ask for advice on something so personal and important. Without knowing a single thing about my business or how I made money, he felt he could trust me.

Second, I couldn't help but be struck by the irony. With all the millionaire members of the Harvard Club, the person potentially offering me a huge opportunity was the waiter. I had developed a relationship with him without expecting anything in return, and there he was offering to give my fund $35 million. Our relationship was able to grow because I treated him as an equal. Ultimately, I was grateful for the opportunity . . . but I didn't take his money.

"Listen, I'm not the right guy to manage your money because you need a more customized financial plan given your situation," I told him. "But I know someone who can help you." I put him in touch with Gerry Kaminsky—who at the time was at Neuberger Berman— and who happened to be both a friend and someone I knew would do a good, honest job for the family. For Neuberger Berman, the situation also served as a case study in the power of a referral. The firm took care of him, and soon enough I stopped seeing my favorite worker in the halls of the Harvard Club.

The moral of the story, and the lesson in this chapter, is simple— treat people well regardless of their position and profession. After all, you never know where you will meet your next client.

Chapter 15

Be Bold—Marketing Takes Courage

Standing Out by Sticking Your Neck Out

"Success is walking from failure to failure with no loss of enthusiasm."
—*Winston Churchill*

The asset management industry has never been more competitive. When I started working in finance more than 27 years ago, there were really only a handful of widely respected asset managers and hedge funds dominating the space. Today, there are hundreds of companies vying for your capital. Thirty years ago, investors had longer attention spans and were willing to give a trusted manager the benefit of the doubt if he had a bad year or two. Today, people are only long-term investors until they experience short-term losses. When things go south, they make knee-jerk decisions, often selling out of asset classes at exactly the wrong time. It's like the lines in the supermarket. We always think we are waiting on the longest line and have an itch to move. The fact that it might always be better to stick to the plan is lost in the current culture of micro-attention. One bad year can cause long-time investors to start seeking redemptions and inhibit a manager's ability to let long-term ideas play out.

In today's fickle and crowded landscape, there are only two ways to separate yourself from the pack: consistent performance and good marketing.

In the same way mediocre performance isn't enough to stand out in this day and age, neither is vanilla marketing. While the temptation exists for many firms to avoid the press, I believe that this play-it-safe approach is detrimental to your business. Whenever you stick your neck out by going on TV, writing op-eds, or by hosting an investment seminar, the positive externalities from those bold efforts dramatically outweigh any potential negative side effects. That said, when constructing these marketing efforts, you must always remain extremely focused on maintaining the ethical and regulatory integrity of your business to ensure that you will never impair your firm's name.

■ ■ ■

Some people say that there is a difference between messaging and publicity. The story goes that you have to carefully measure what people say about you and do your best to control it. I do not believe or subscribe to that theory. The best we can do in an age of social media is to make sure we are out there allowing for a personalization of our businesses. The more that we can share our stories, the harder it is for people to criticize or demonize.

I once heard a story about the insurance company Aflac that resonated with me. In 1990, Daniel P. Amos took over as the CEO of the American Family Life Assurance Company. He immediately set about restructuring the company, closing underperforming units, and increasing the focus on the core brands in both Japan and the United States.

Despite being one of the largest insurance companies in the world, internal polling revealed the company was only recognized by a paltry 2 percent of the U.S. population. Why? Well, for starters, the name was too generic; there were dozens of other insurance companies starting with the word American. So, instead of going through the laborious process of changing its name, he simply shortened it to the more memorable acronym, Aflac.

With a memorable company name established, Amos also set out to create an ad campaign that would increase brand awareness. The company worked with a number of different ad agencies, reviewing hundreds of pitches. Eventually, management narrowed it down to two concepts. The first included Ray Romano, who at the time was the highly recognizable star of the hit sitcom *Everybody Loves Raymond*. The ad, which included him spelling out the company's name with a bunch of school children, tested reasonably well, with around 20 percent of people who saw the commercial remembering the company's name.

The other ad was something completely different. New York–based agency Kaplan Thaler Group came up with this concept of an Aflac duck that would quack the word *Aflac* over and over again in the commercial. The ad guys actually stumbled upon the idea when they were having a hard time remembering the name of the firm. "What's the name again of the firm we're pitching?" one executive asked. "For the last time, it's Aflac, Aflac, Aflac!" a fellow worker responded. Another person in the room remarked that he sounded like a duck, and the rest was history.

The duck commercial tested off the chart. Everyone who saw the ad remembered the name of the company, which was the ultimate goal.

Amos had a tough decision. Go with the safe ad with the big star favored by most of the company's management, or the bolder, riskier campaign that could be a game changer.

Amos sought advice from outside parties, trying to explain the two concepts, but once he started talking about the duck, he got a lot of blank stares.

However, in his gut Amos knew he was sitting on something special. On New Year's Day 2000, the first Aflac duck spot debuted on

CNN. Aflac choose CNN because of the network's nonstop coverage of Y2K hysteria that was sure to attract business viewers.

The ad campaign was a smashing success. Aflac's web site got more hits on the first day of the ads than it had in the entire year prior. Kids started asking for stuffed Aflac ducks. People loved, hated, mocked, and praised the spot, but at the very least it generated tremendous buzz.

Most importantly, the campaign had an immediate transformative effect on the company's bottom line. Sales in the United States jumped 29 percent a year after the ads debuted. Three years later, they doubled. Much of it was due to an increase in name recognition, which jumped 67 percent two years after the first ad aired. Aflac always had a valued product, but without brand awareness it was like a tree falling in an empty forest.

■ ■ ■

Creative marketing efforts can propel your business to the next level. I know they have for SkyBridge.

To be an effective marketer, you have to be willing to take chances and to live with the consequences of those decisions. There will always be journalists and Internet trolls who take a dim view of you and your business. Who cares? Fight through that anxiety and self-consciousness to be bold.

At SkyBridge, we are doing everything in our power to move the company forward, ensure that our message doesn't get stale, and continuously hop over any rabbit holes that we may stumble upon. The competition is fierce, and at the end of the day, you need to convince someone why your firm is different and worth their money. Be creative and bold, get over mistakes quickly, and apply skin thickener every day.

Here are four rules to help you boldly—and, somewhat, unconventionally—market your firm to your target audience.

Rule 1: Get Out There and Talk to the Press

I'm not sure when the tradition started, but somewhere along the way financial firms started thinking that being in the press was a bad thing. Money managers hired public relations firms to keep them out of the news and away from reporters. In my opinion, that is a completely backwards approach. If you become a meaningful player in the industry, the press is going to cover you one way or another. Define the narrative; don't let it define you. The best way to shape the media's view of you is to engage them. Appearing on television and being quoted in stories only reinforces your credibility.

At SkyBridge, we've taken a more proactive approach to engaging the media. I don't want to be in the flyover section, where someone looks at my company's logo and simply turns the page. I want to be the native content. I want to be in the story. The same applies to television.

In the SALT profile in the *New York Times,* author Peter Lattman described the conference as a "Wall Street schmooze-fest." He wrote about the great guests, fabulous entertainers, and overall fun factor of the conference. He credited "irrepressible salesmanship" for the explosive growth of SkyBridge, articulating our strategy of going after the mass affluent. And to balance out the article, he talked about the difficult environment for hedge funds, the standard criticism over fees.

Having the *New York Times* write about your organization or business initiative—whether good, bad, or indifferent—is the greatest ad campaign of all-time, and it doesn't cost a dime. Lattman is one of the toughest reporters out there, which is why the article tremendously boosted our credibility. It was the type of content money can't buy because it came from a respected, objective journalist. None of it would have been possible if I hadn't engaged the press. There have been others who haven't been so kind, but those articles boosted our profile, too.

Rule 2: Focus on What Makes You Different

In *The Art of War*, Sun Tzu famously says, "Appear weak when you are strong, and strong when you are weak." Although he wasn't talking about marketing when he wrote those words, it happens to be applicable and practical advice when designing a communications campaign. Because what he was really talking about was the image that one projects in the world, and how to turn weakness into strength. Anything can be turned into an advantage if you're willing to think positively. Think your business is small? No, it's nimble. Your company is too young? No, it's disruptive. The best way to market your business is to zero in on your competitive advantages.

When Richard Branson started Virgin Airlines, he didn't try to compete on price with Pan Am or British Air. Instead, he focused on what made his airline different: the great service, legroom, plush seats, sleek cabins, and in-flight bar. As discussed in Chapter 5, Branson brought back the glory days of flying, harkening back to a time when air travel was glamorous and enjoyable.

And how did he raise awareness of his company? Well, let's just say he didn't buy banner ads. He flew around the world in a hot air balloon, he bungee-jumped off the side of the Palms Hotel Casino (bumping into the building twice and tearing his pants in the process).

The publicity stunts had nothing to do with his airline company, but it told people, "Hey, we're different. We're not afraid to try new things." And it worked. Virgin America became one of the most popular airlines in the country before its sale to Alaska Airlines in 2016. It's the anti-airline, the one you always check on when you're getting set to travel.

Whatever business you're in, don't follow the status quo. Come up with original ideas to solve problems for customers, and constantly highlight the differentiating factor that separates you from your competitors.

At SkyBridge, we know that we are not BlackRock, Fidelity, or Goldman Sachs. We don't have 80 years of history and tradition, so we have to excel in other areas and differentiate ourselves from our industry peers. One thing that makes us unique in the alternative investments space is that we've opened up the rarified air of hedge funds to the mass affluent. If endowments and institutions have access to the sophisticated strategies of legendary hedge funds, why shouldn't mass affluent investors? Our approach to marketing underscores that mentality. We meet people face-to-face. We communicate openly and honestly. And we aren't afraid to disrupt the status quo and try new things.

Rule 3: Use Nontraditional Marketing Tools to Get Your Message Out

At SkyBridge, we often use untraditional marketing means. So how do we get that message out?

We throw a massive conference in Las Vegas bringing together thought leaders and influencers across all industries, from Wall Street to Hollywood to politics to technology to sports. Hedge fund investors and financial advisers get the opportunity to rub elbows with Magic Johnson and Mike Krzyzewski, Mark Cuban, Al Pacino, and Kevin Spacey.

Rather than spend ad dollars on boring marketing campaigns, we sponsored a public bike-sharing program in West Palm Beach that is similar to Citibike in New York. Did we expect people to rent a bike for the day in Palm Beach and then immediately open an account with SkyBridge? Of course not. But we thought it was a worthwhile venture for building brand awareness in an area in which we were actively penetrating . . . and it even got us an above-the-fold feature article in the *Wall Street Journal*.

In 2015, we also revived *Wall Street Week*, the most iconic financial television show of all time. The show, hosted by Louis Rukeyser on PBS for 35 years, had a tradition of hosting thoughtful, big-picture discussions about the economy and financial markets, something we thought was missing from today's landscape of loud, hysterical, short-term-oriented financial media. We took a creative approach to distributing the show, buying time in major markets in order to maintain digital distribution rights. We allowed consumers the flexibility to watch the show on YouTube and Facebook, or to listen to it as a podcast. We launched a newsletter to provide a comprehensive weekly recap of financial markets, as well as dive deeper into important topics discussed on the show each week. The over-the-top approach was a smashing success, and the show was picked by Fox after several networks expressed interest. Reviving *Wall Street Week* helped us to further reinforce our credibility and creative mind-set.

All of these efforts together have helped create a charismatic brand that is truly unique within the industry. It all starts with a strong investment team and good performance and proceeds with an ability to attract customers. People want to be a part of the SkyBridge movement, and I can assure you we are just getting started in terms of pursuing creative projects.

Rule 4: Take a Portfolio Manager's Approach to Marketing

Just as every stock in your portfolio won't go up all the time, not every marketing idea works. When you're trying to think outside the box and be creative, it's inevitable you'll have missteps along the way. As with investing, the important thing is that you recognize a loser early and cut bait. However, fear of failure shouldn't prevent you from taking chances. It simply means you have to hedge your bets. In other words, you need to manage your marketing efforts in much the same way you approach asset allocation in a portfolio.

A good portfolio manager doesn't concentrate his investments in only a few ideas. The objective is to build strategy based on the current environment that is able to come out ahead of a benchmark. The core of your portfolio should be steady blue-chip stocks and investment-grade credit. Build a strong sales team. Have killer customer service. Put together a great investor relations team. Get your company branding right. But in order to beat the benchmark and gain a step on your competition, you also have to take a set of calculated, contrarian risks.

As a marketer, you need to take the same approach. Diversify your marketing efforts among traditional and nontraditional strategies in order to reach your goals. If you start with a great product and take a bold but balanced approach to marketing, you're going to be successful.

Conclusion

I Am Enough

"The successful man is not so superior in ability as in action."
—*Roger Babson*

"Are you nervous?" my friend asked.

"Nervous?" I replied, looking out at the field as my daughter, Amelia, walked up to the mound. "No, I'm excited!"

That was only half true. I was terrified, but in a good way. I was excited, nervous, thrilled, exhilarated, and scared . . . all at the same time.

My beautiful daughter, Amelia, was marching to home plate at Shea Stadium to sing "God Bless America" for the seventh-inning stretch. It was July 27, 2008, and I was giving her the ultimate gift. I'm not talking about the opportunity to sing at Shea. It was something better. At the age of 12 she was learning a great lesson about overcoming your fears.

Like many young women, my daughter wants to be a professional entertainer. The difference is how seriously she takes her talent. She works at her craft 24/7. She practices all the time with voice and singing coaches, studying other singers the way law students prepare for the bar exam. But like a lot of young people, she occasionally gets nervous in front of big crowds. I wanted to help her conquer that fear and give her the gift of self-confidence. If she could nail "God Bless America" in front of 50,000 people, she would never lack the poise to perform in front of a crowd again.

"You have a great voice. You want to do this for a living." I told her one day. "I'm going to get you in front of the crowd at Shea Stadium, and you're going to perform. And you're going to learn how to perform under pressure."

Amelia had done school plays and concerts before. But nothing close to this magnitude. She let out a shriek and threw her arms around me, exclaiming, "Dad, this is great. I am going to work at this and do my best!"

If you have kids, you know the drill—one second you're a hero, the next you're the bad guy. It's always tempting to spoil your kids so they'll love you all the time, but you have to resist the temptation. It's hard, and I certainly have not gotten the balance right all the time. The greatest gifts you can give your children are not material possessions but rather opportunities to grow and learn . . . and, of course, unconditional love.

It took only a couple of days, though, for her gratitude to morph into trepidation.

"Daddy, I can't do it," she said in her most dramatic voice. "What if I clam up?"

"Amelia, you're going to be great."

"It's too many people. I can't do this."

"Amelia, listen to me. This is really important. You're twelve years old. If you can pull this off, you'll never have stage fright again. You'll be able to face anything. I want to give you the gift of self-confidence, and this is the best way to do it."

■■■

Most people hate public speaking. It brings out a sense of anxiety and self-loathing, and a fear of failure that's hard to replicate in any other setting. I've seen brilliant people turn into incoherent babblers on stage and PhDs sound like kindergartners. Once you've had that first stressful experience in front of a crowd, it further increases the sense of fear and dread you feel when preparing for a big speech, performance, or presentation. Like everything, however, with enough practice and discipline, you can get better at it and become a public speaking maven.

If you want to be a successful entrepreneur, you must get comfortable with the idea of public speaking. Although I enjoy it now, it wasn't always that way. I had to train myself to be good at it. Below are some tips.

People Are Just People

I knew just the trick, which would also help Amelia deal with her nerves.

"Just imagine you're singing to me," I told her.

The collective stare of a large crowd feels like a 500-pound weight on your chest, but you can reduce the anxiety by focusing on the fact that a crowd is just a collection of individuals. If you were asked to speak in front of one person, you probably wouldn't be quite as nervous. When you are in a room full of hundreds or thousands of people and you find yourself becoming overwhelmed with anxiety, simply zero in on one person in the crowd. Think about singing to one person, 50,000 times.

Make Eye Contact

The more personal you make a conversation, the more relaxed you will become. When I go on TV, I make a point of looking directly into the eyes of the host or guest, and if I'm speaking into the camera I pretend my wife is on the other side. When I'm speaking in front of a crowd, I basically pick out a few people in the audience with whom to have a conversation. The more you narrow your focus visually, the greater your mental sharpness.

The most important quality you can have as a public figure is authenticity. The camera can always tell when you're faking it. The camera highlights your issues, especially the ones you have with yourself.

Practice Like You Play

As a sophomore in high school, Michael Jordan was cut from his varsity basketball team. Yet through his determination, strong work ethic, and practice habits, he later developed into one of the greatest basketball players—and athletes—of all. He used to go at his teammates every day as if it were game seven of the NBA finals.

"Work eliminates fear," Jordan once said. "When the game came, I wasn't nervous because there was nothing I hadn't already practiced."

Like many great athletes and successful entrepreneurs, Jordan was fueled by people telling him he couldn't do something. He practiced so tirelessly that when big moments arrived and he looked across at his opponents, he knew they couldn't possibly be more prepared than he was. The best way to conquer anxiety is to overprepare. Practice as if you're playing a championship game, and play the championship game as if it is practice.

When you're preparing to give a speech or performance, rehearse until it becomes second nature. Solicit honest feedback from friends, family, and colleagues. Encourage people to be critical. When it comes time for the big moment, there should be no doubt in your mind that you are prepared.

Amelia overcame her anxiety about performing at the Mets game by preparing her heart out. She spent hours and hours practicing in front of the mirror and small groups. She went to Shea Stadium to get comfortable standing on the mound. The audio system at Shea had been in place since the 1960s, and as a result there was a three-second echo from the mic to the speakers. She practiced getting used to that. She practiced her walk out to home plate, complete with the wave to the crowds. She familiarized herself with the green room, the makeup counter, and the bathroom. By the time she was done, she could have made her way around the stadium blindfolded. Could she have delivered a great performance without doing all this? Probably. But if you want to be great, you can leave no stone unturned.

■■■

The big day arrived and Amelia could not have been more excited. It was the type of eager nervousness that comes with great preparation. If you sing the national anthem, you get it over with at the beginning of the game, but when you're singing during the seventh-inning stretch, you have the whole game to let your anxiety marinate.

It was a hot day, and the sky looked like it could break at any moment. By the fifth inning, I was worried she would get rained out. The weather held off, though, and I made my way down with her to the green room and then out on the field. I stood along the first base line as she strode confidently to the home plate.

"Please welcome, from Manhasset, New York, Amelia Scaramucci for the singing of 'God Bless America.'"

Applause. An elegant wave and then a big smile from Amelia. She took the mic, the crowd grew silent, and for a brief moment, my heart stopped.

"Goooooddddd bless America. Lannnnnd that I love."

My heart melted. At that moment I could not be prouder. How did we manage to raise such a brave and beautiful daughter?

"... God bless America, my hooooome sweet hooooome."

The crowd erupted in cheers. Amelia clapped her hand to her face, waving and blowing kisses to the crowd. She absolutely crushed it, just like she practiced.

Afterwards, she ran up to me in tears. The pure adrenaline of the moment practically had her shaking. It is such a proud moment for me that each time I think about, even years later, my heart wants to explode.

On the car ride home, I could barely contain my enthusiasm.

"Do you realize how incredible you were up there?"

"Thanks, Dad." But at this point, much of the adrenaline had already left her system. She was on to the next event in her life, texting her friends and planning the weekend.

"Do you realize you can look back at this moment and say 'I crushed it in front of 50,000 people at Shea?' You'll never be nervous again."

She looked back at me with a sweet and gracious smile.

"Were you nervous?" I asked.

"Maybe at first. But once I was out there, not really."

"Why not?"

"Because at the end of the day, Daddy, I know that I am enough."

Sometimes kids say the most profound things. Those moments are particularly meaningful when it's your own children doing the talking. Amelia might have been talking about her nerve to sing in front of a packed stadium, but she had unknowingly dispensed the greatest advice any entrepreneur could ever hear.

If you don't believe you are enough, you're never going to get to where you want to be. Entrepreneurship is a form of artistry, and being an artist requires belief. Success requires luck, opportunism, and a dollop of intelligence, but more than anything, it requires conviction that you will do what it takes to get the job done. That you will courageously stare the inevitable failures in the face and strategically hop over the many rabbit holes that you will encounter. The hard work and tireless commitment should never stop. That is the essence of this book. It is your attitude that will make you.

Start a business. Follow your dreams. I promise, if you put your mind to it, you'll be enough.

Acknowledgments

These are always tricky to write, as invariably, someone is unintentionally left out and there is a potential for hurt feelings. I still laugh when I recall David M. Darst—my friend and colleague—sending the phonebook to his publisher for his acknowledgments when he wrote his bestselling books. "Anthony, it is for people to see their name in print and hopefully go out and buy the book!" It was a good strategy, but I will keep mine to an Academy Awards acceptance speech level of length.

I want to thank my Mom and Dad—Al and Marie Scaramucci—for raising me and putting me in the position to excel in life. They are basically a cheerleading squad and support group rolled into one. They did their best, so now I am tasked with trying to do mine. My wonderful wife, Deidre, for being kind and loving, and for helping me put down my phone and focus on being present. My children—AJ, Amelia, Anthony, and Nicholas—for being in my life; my bet is you aren't responsible for that, but you are however, responsible for a good part of your own destinies so I want to thank all of you for being so wonderful. Additionally, I would like to thank my mom-in-law, June Ball, for accepting me in the family and loving me like a son.

I also want to thank Andrew K. Boszhardt Jr., who was a senior partner at Oscar Capital Management, a firm I helped start in December 1996. He has been an incredible mentor and friend. Without his help, I probably wouldn't have had the courage to leave Goldman. Andy, I will always be grateful to you. Your support is one of the crucial elements behind whatever success I have experienced.

At SkyBridge Capital, I'd like to thank all of my partners and colleagues for their hard work, commitment, and dedication to excellence. I am certain that together we can tackle any business challenge and thrive.

The Fox Business and Fox News Channel teams have taught me a lot about being on the air and doing it in a world class way. Bill Shine, Jack Abernethy, Suzanne Scott, Dianne Brandi, Irene Briganti and Caley Cronin, Megan Brown, Gary Schrier, Brian Jones, and their production teams. On the talent side there are so many people to acknowledge including Maria Bartiromo, Liz Claman, Trish Regan, Deirdre Bolton, David Asman, Neil Cavuto, Charlie Gasparino (who helped me to land at Fox), Sean Hannity, Stuart Varney, Lou Dobbs, and Charles Payne. They are all the best at what they do and, as Yogi Berra said (and I am paraphrasing), "You can learn a lot by watching."

My deep thanks to the creative minds who helped me with the manuscript and encouraged me throughout this process. My former CNBC colleague Max Meyers was instrumental in the early drafts of this book and I am grateful for his wisdom and insight. John Darsie has been a real force of nature in our business. He is a great writer who has found my voice and enabled me to look like I am appearing in more places than one. Debby Englander, who is a true pro in this business and guided me along the way. To the terrific team at John Wiley & Sons, including Joan O'Neil, Laura Gachko, Tula Weis, Mike Henton, and Steve Kyritz. And, a deep thanks to Victor Oviedo, Susan Krakower, Eric Alper, Jessica Levin, Samantha Darsie, Jennifer Connelly, and the JConnelly team who have been incredible with their time and support.

I would be remiss if I didn't give a shout-out to Kelly O'Connor. Kelly has worked on all three of my books and is a brilliant writer and editor. I appreciate her guidance and honest feedback. When she told me the first draft of *Goodbye Gordon Gekko* was terrible more than six years ago, I knew I had to bring her over to SkyBridge.

Like any Oscar speech, I am certain that I have left someone out, but I want to thank you from the bottom of my heart. We are only as good as the people we associate ourselves with and I can assure you that you have added to my life and for this I am very grateful.

About the Author

Anthony Scaramucci
*Founder & Co-Managing Partner, SkyBridge Capital and Co-Host of
"Wall Street Week"*

Anthony Scaramucci is the founder and co-managing partner of SkyBridge Capital, a global investment firm with around $12.5 billion in assets under management and advisement as of August 1, 2016. The firm also produces the annual SkyBridge Alternatives ("SALT") Conference, a premier global investment and thought leadership forum.

Mr. Scaramucci is co-host of *Wall Street Week*, the iconic financial television show that was revived in 2015, as well as a contributor to the Fox Business Network and Fox News Channel. He is the author of two books: *The Little Book of Hedge Funds* and *Goodbye Gordon Gekko*. Mr. Scaramucci also hosts a podcast on entrepreneurship called "The Motivation Inside (TMI)."

Prior to founding SkyBridge in 2005, Mr. Scaramucci co-founded investment partnership Oscar Capital Management, which was sold to Neuberger Berman in 2001. Earlier, Mr. Scaramucci was a vice president in Private Wealth Management at Goldman Sachs.

In 2015, Mr. Scaramucci was ranked #91 in *Worth* magazine's Power 100: The 100 Most Powerful People in Global Finance. In 2011, he received Ernst & Young's Entrepreneur of the Year New York Award in the Financial Services category.

Mr. Scaramucci is a member of the Council on Foreign Relations (CFR), vice chair of the Kennedy Center Corporate Fund Board, board member of the Brain Tumor Foundation and Business Executives for National Security (BENS), trustee of the United States Olympic and Paralympic Foundation, and member of the Tufts University Fletcher School of Law and Diplomacy Board of Advisors. Mr. Scaramucci is also an active bundler within the Republican Party, having served on the national campaign finance committees for Mitt Romney and Donald Trump.

Mr. Scaramucci, a native of Long Island, New York, holds a B.A. in Economics from Tufts University and a J.D. from Harvard Law School.

Index